# Kingston Second to None

### by
### Don Curtis

A study and discussion of the outstanding opportunities available to Kingston, Ontario, Canada. Opportunities for the most part missed, underappreciated, underpromoted, and undervalued.

Copyright © 2014 DON CURTIS

All rights reserved.

ISBN-13: 978-1503021877
ISBN-10: 1503021874

# DEDICATION

## This book is dedicated to
## The City of Kingston, Ontario, Canada.

ABOUT THE AUTHOR --

DON CURTIS IS A RETIRED MARKETING /COMMUNICATIONS PROFESSIONAL WHO MOVED TO KINGSTON IN 2000 AND, FOR THE PAST 14 YEARS, HAS BEEN STUDYING AND WRITING ABOUT THE CITY AND ITS HISTORIC AND WATER ASSETS.

ASSETS -- AS YOU WILL READ -- THAT MAKE THE CITY OF KINGSTON SECOND TO NONE AS A PLACE TO LIVE, WORK, PLAY AND RETIRE.

KINGSTON HAS ACHIEVED THE MAGIC BALANCE OF
QUALITY OF PLACE WITH QUALITY OF PACE

# Foreword

In 1673, Count Frontenac, the Governor of New France, chose the site of the future Kingston to build a fort and trading post at the confluence of the Cataraqui River, the St. Lawrence River and Lake Ontario. He chose wisely. The site provided vital transportation routes for trade and commerce, for defence and for exploration of the new world. In ensuing years, the site would house Fort Henry and the southern end of the Rideau Canal and play a key role in securing the preservation of Canada as a nation during the War of 1812. It provided major maritime commerce for the growth of the country and built ships for three wars. Kingston would subsequently become the home of Canada's first Prime Minister, the site of Canada's oldest degree-granting university, and the first capital of our nation. I believe that Confucius was right when he said, "Study the past if you would define the future." But today there is much more to Kingston than our rich history.

Kingston, sometimes referred to as the "windy city", is now recognized as the fresh water sailing capital of the world. Situated between the Cataraqui and St. Lawrence Rivers, Lake Ontario and 5,000 lakes to our north, we live in a proverbial "Blue Belt" with unique sailing, diving, fishing and paddling opportunities. And our downtown core has been developed in an environmentally-sensitive and aesthetically-pleasing manner, with a view to making our City a national jewel at the northeastern tip of Lake Ontario. In sum, Kingston offers both residents and tourists a superb quality of life - second to none. It is one of the reasons why, having seen how people live in more than 60 countries around the world in my nearly 40 years in the Canadian Army, I have chosen to settle in Kingston. Sadly, our marketing efforts have not been optimized and few Kingstonians appreciate how lucky they really are.

As a communications and marketing professional, copy writer and strategic planner with over 40 years in the Canadian advertising industry, handling many of Canada's largest companies and an avid history buff, Don Curtis has given significant thought to what makes Kingston inimitable in Canada and how the City can reach its full potential as the destination of choice to visit, live, work, play and retire.

In this inspired account -- *"Kingston Second to None"* -- he succinctly articulates the dozens of reasons why Canadians and visitors from all over the world should include Kingston as a "must do" stop in their travel plans. He has provided the vision and the road map. It now behooves the various organizations and attraction stakeholders to better integrate and market their brand through innovative, collaborative programs and to effectively use the web-based technologies, consistent with the City of Kingston's Official And Cultural Plans.

We have an opportunity to build upon Don Curtis' visionary insights and take a leadership role in building a better future for our historic and beautiful city --- we have no alternative but to forge ahead.

**Serge Labbe, Brigadier General (retired), Canadian Army**

*"We often miss opportunities because they arrive looking like work." -- Thomas Edison*

# CONTENTS

## Section 1 -- Introduction ….. 1

Chapter 1: Kingston2nd2none ….. 3
Chapter 2: Kingston Facts ….. 5
Chapter 3: The Brand ….. 7
Chapter 4: Hiding Our Light Under a Barrel ….. 11
Chapter 5: Vision ….. 13
Chapter 6: An Economic Development Discussion ….. 15

## Section 2 -- History and Heritage ….. 21

Chapter 7: The Historic Heart of Canada ….. 23
Chapter 8: The King Street Experience ….. 27
Chapter 9: The Stories and Storeys of Store Street ….. 37
Chapter 10: Kingston and The War of 1812 ….. 47
Chapter 11: Cast of Characters ….. 57
Chapter 12: www.HistoryMoments.ca ….. 81
Chapter 13: The Loyalist Parkway /
Birth of a Nation ….. 85

## Section 3 -- Water, Water Everywhere ….. 91

Chapter 14: Kingston's Blue Belt ….. 93
Chapter 15: Kingston's Other Waterfront ….. 111
Chapter 16: Land o' Lakes / Frontenac County ….. 119
Chapter 17: The Marine Museum
of the Great Lakes ….. 127

## Section 4 -- The City ..... 135

Chapter 18: Hockey: The Great Frozen Game ..... 137
Chapter 19: Kingston Downtown Ideas ..... 143
Chapter 20: Over 500 Things To Do, To Join, To Learn, and Participate In ..... 149
Chapter 21: The Silver Lining is Tinged with Grey ..... 157
Chapter 22: Kingston2nd2none - Review ..... 163

## Section 5 -- The Summary ..... 165

Chapter 23: Summary of Opportunities ..... 167
Chapter 24: Conclusion ..... 171

References ..... 75

# Section 1
# Introduction

# Chapter 1
# Kingston2nd2none

On the following pages, the author endeavours to show why Kingston is 2nd2none as a place to live, work and play. For whatever reasons, our considerable assets as a city remain underappreciated, underpromoted and undervalued. Other Canadian cities would covet any of these assets. Collectively, these assets represent millions of potential dollars in tourism, in economic development, and in the growth of the city and its tax base.

**We are the historic heart of Canada.** A statement and fact that represents a goldmine of tourist opportunities.

**A war was fought here.** A major tourist draw everywhere in the world. Gettysburg, Virginia celebrates a three-day battle of their Civil War, generating $95 million yearly.

**A nation was built here.**

**We are the Fresh Water Sailing Capital of the World.** If an American city could make this claim, there would be signs in all directions for 100 kilometres, but there is no sign on the 401, no sign in Confederation Park, no sign at Portsmouth Olympic Harbour.

**Kingston is surrounded by fresh, blue water, giving us a lifestyle that is the envy of any other city.** The Kingston Blue Belt represents our greatest asset for tourism and for economic development, as it delivers a water/recreational lifestyle sought after by the young, active and well educated, technological workforce.

**We are a fishermen's paradise, a paddler's dream, and a hiker's delight.** These facts go unnoticed.

**We are 30 minutes from Canada's most southerly wilderness park.**

**We have 5,000 bodies of water to our north.** If you fished a different one of our lakes each week, it would take 96 years to fish them all. And our neighbours to the south spend $40 billion dollars annually on fishing. There are 38 lakes within a one hour drive of City Hall alone.

**We have hundreds of sunken ships -- a virtual underwater museum to the maritime history of the Great Lakes.** Wrecks include the "*St. Lawrence*", the largest warship ever built on the lakes. Yet, this goldmine for divers is hardly even mentioned on U.S. dive websites.

**We are a city of historic firsts.**

**We have 600 heritage buildings in our core**, each with a fantastic story of its own. History and heritage sell. ALL over the world.

*Luck is a matter of preparation meets opportunity.*

**During the War of 1812 - known as the Shipbuilder's War - 15 major battleships were built in Kingston.** We need to celebrate this heritage. **Famous and historically significant people strode our streets.** Count Frontenac, Sieur de La Salle, Molly Brant, United Empire Loyalists, John Stuart, Lord Sydenham, Billy Bishop and, of course, Sir John A. Macdonald -- yet, there is no museum to any of the above. We have Sir John's office chair! Imagine if the U.S. had George Washington's chair -- it would be enshrined and on display for $25 a person.

**TV vignettes featuring Kingston history attracted 1,000,000 viewings in just 90 days, making it the fastest growing history website in the world.** History sells all over the world. These viewings are worth over $20 million in media exposure and at not one penny cost to the city.

**Land o' Lakes is truly Eastern Canada's Outdoor Playground and itself represents a tourism goldmine if branded and promoted.**

**15,000,000 cars pass by Kingston on the 401 each year.**

**We are the cradle of hockey.** The subject dearest to Canadian hearts -- and we have a fantastic story to tell! Yet, we hide a small sample away north of the city. Another lost tourism opportunity.

**We have an untapped reservoir of intellectual capital.** Queen's University, the Royal Military College, St. Lawrence College, retired executives, retired professors, retired senior military officers -- intellectual capital that could be highly effective in attracting businesses to the area. But none are called upon.

**We have a vibrant downtown with an active music scene.** A huge draw for young people.

**Each year, hundreds of senior executives come to Kingston.** But we put nothing in their hands to tell them about the assets of Kingston to live, work, play and invest...hundreds of opportunities lost for the $1 cost of a CD-ROM.

**We have all the amenities to attract super seniors to retire here.** People selling their million dollar homes in Toronto, Montreal and Ottawa, and who are looking for a better lifestyle...looking for a place exactly like Kingston, where there is a Quality of Place with a Quality of Pace.

**We have all the amenities to attract a young, active educated workforce.**
**We have all the amenities to attract businesses.**


Kingston truly is 2nd2none. We merely have to tell our stories to the world, and the world will beat a path to our door.

# Chapter 2
# Kingston Facts

*Kingston is the Fresh Water Sailing Capital of the World.
*Kingston is the oldest city in Ontario.
*Kingston has the oldest farmers' market in Canada.
*Kingston was the first Capital of Canada.
*Sir John A. Macdonald, Canada's First Prime Minister, was raised, worked in, and is buried in Kingston.
*73% of Kingston's workforce has a post-secondary degree.
*Queen's University is the oldest degree-granting university in Canada.
*The Kingston Whig Standard is the oldest daily newspaper in Canada.
*The Kingston Police Force is the country's oldest law enforcement agency.
*Kingston is home to the only UNESCO heritage designated sites in Ontario.
*Kingston is surrounded by fresh water.
*Kingston is the birthplace of the Ontario brewing industry.
*Kingston has 600 heritage buildings in its downtown core -- all still in use.
*Kingston is home to North America's oldest operating $19^{th}$ Century canal.
*Kingston has some of the bests hiking in Ontario, just 30 minutes from the city in Canada's most southerly wilderness park.
*The Kingston region is home to 350 species of birds, including Bald Eagles and Snowy Owls.
*There is a virtual underwater museum of sunken ships right off shore.
*Kingston was the site of the 1976 Olympic sailing races.
*Kingston is home to CORK, the Canadian Olympic Regatta.
*Upper and Lower Canada were united in Kingston.
*The first two Governor Generals of Canada died in Kingston.
*The first session of Canadian Parliament took place in Kingston.
*Winston Churchill visited Kingston two times: 1901 and 1940.
* Kingston is the site of the first Catholic school west of Quebec.
*St. George's Cathedral is the founding church of the Anglican religion in Canada.
*Billy Bishop, World War I flying ace, attended RMC in Kingston.
*RMC graduated the first Canadian military officers.
*Kingston had the first protestant cemetery in Canada.

**All the more testament to Kingston2nd2none!**

# Chapter 3
# The Brand

## Everything has a brand image -- whether it wants one or not

If everything has a brand image, what is Kingston's? And what would we want it to be if we could change it? Two important questions, and the answers are critical to the success of the city in the future.

Kingston's current image depends on who you ask. People coming to the city for the first time describe it as a beautiful place with fine old buildings, great architecture, universities and sailing. Not a bad start. But corporations looking to build have all but ignored the city.

Residents recognize both of the above, and describe the city as " The Tale of Two Cities" (note: this data is derived from over 200 in-person interviews by the author.)

On the one hand, the city is seen as serene, beautiful, well-educated, quaint, historic, safe, easy to get around. On the other hand, it is described as asleep at the wheel of progress, shut off from its potential, stuffy, stuck in the status quo, having a do-nothing philosophy and afraid of change.

**In both cases, they are correct.**

Many residents like the city the way it is and shun the idea of growth. Others are frustrated that the city's enormous potential goes to waste, unfulfilled and unrealized. Why the frustration? We have three institutes of higher learning, three hospitals, a major military base -- all stabilizing our economy. The above institutions are headed by capable, bright individuals who are very committed to the city.

The city needs a vision for its future.

What do the citizens of Kingston want it to be? Kingstonians love their city and don't really want it to change its core values. We are -- and want to remain -- the product of our Loyalist roots. We like the way the city looks and moves, we like its water lifestyle, its quaintness, its ambiance, its intellectualism that Queen's University and the Royal Military College impart to us. In many ways, we are a well-kept secret and some want to keep it that way. Others want to enjoy the services and extras that growth will bring, and they want to be proud of the city's successes and its uniqueness. We should be the envy of every other city in the country. The fact that we are not speaks volumes. We have slammed the door on opportunity and potential.

**We must ask ourselves why???**

Kingston does not make the top 40 places in Canada to do business. Our student housing ranks 38th. We are not on the radar of major corporations, yet the heads of many of Canada's leading companies are Queen's graduates, and hundreds of executives pass through the city every year (Queen's MBA and the Donald Gordon Centre) and we put nothing in their hands about Kingston as a potential place of business. A great DVD would do wonders.

*15,000,000 cars pass by Kingston on the 401 each year (that's about 21,000,000 people = 21,000,000 potential shoppers and tourists) but we don't speak to them.
*We have the finest water lifestyle in North America.
*We have the most southerly wilderness park in Canada just 30 minutes away.
*The young, well educated workforce is moving to markets that offer outdoor lifestyles like ours.
*We have three hospitals, the Cancer Research Institute, and Kingston General Hospital is the only teaching hospital in a mid-sized market in Canada.
*We have Queen's University, the Royal Military College and St. Lawrence College -- the #1 economic development trend is to markets offering Education and Medicine (Eds & Meds) as a base...Exactly what we have.
* We are consistently ranked in the best downtowns in North America.
*We are only one of four markets in all of Canada with significant 19th Century heritage and the only one west of Quebec.
*There are only a handful of world-class sailing venues in the world, and we are the only one in North America and the only fresh water port.
*We are the site of the first Capital of Canada, site of the first Parliament, the place where Upper and Lower Canada were united.

*We are the place the United Empire Loyalists came to build a new nation, the place where the Anglican faith in Canada started, the home of Sir John A. Macdonald, the first Prime Minister of Canada and the Father of Confederation.
*We are a place of colleges and higher education.
*We are a place of soldiers.
*We are a place of history and heritage.
*We are a place of healthcare.
*We are a place of music.
*We are a place of forests and lakes.
*And we have found the right balance of **Quality of Place with Quality of Pace.**

Let's quickly look at Boom Towns, those markets experiencing significant growth in population and economic development:
*They have a university.
*They have water.
*They have walkable, vibrant downtowns filled with restaurants, pubs and music.
*They have history and heritage.
*They have access to canoeing, hiking, camping, biking, etc.
*They have a host of activities for families and children.

## By all measurements and attributes, Kingston should be a Boom Town!

**Kingston has everything it needs to succeed as the best place in Canada to live, work or play.**
*We need to utilize and maximize our assets for tourism and economic development.
*We need to focus on doing the right things with the right plan of action.
*We need to communicate to the world with one clear voice all that we have to offer.

## Kingston is 2nd2none as a place to live, work and play.

# Key points from Chapter 3

Kingston is a tale of two cities -- one vibrant, one asleep.

We need a vision for our future.

We need new ideas.

We need to communicate our strengths, not only to the outside world, but to our own citizens.

We need to talk to the 15,000,000 people in the cars driving past Kingston on the 401 every year.

We need to talk to the thousands of senior business people who visit our city each year.

We are The Fresh Water Sailing Capital of the World, and we need to brag about that.

We have hundreds of historic buildings and hundreds of stories to tell.

We must promote our assets. Promote our water lifestyle. Promote our history and heritage. They are unique and they are valuable.

We must stop hiding our light under a barrel.

*Opportunities don't knock -- you have to beat down the door.*

# Chapter 4
# Hiding Our Light Under a Barrel
(instead of showcasing our considerable assets)

It is easy to forget or ignore the assets of one's own city. Do Parisians regularly go the Eiffel Tower? No. (But seven million visitors a year do). Do Torontonians visit the CN Tower regularly? No. Do the people of New York visit the Statue of Liberty? No. But they all proudly show them off and make millions in the process.

Kingstonians do little to self-promote the city; in fact, many seem to do the reverse and criticize it on a regular basis. What a shame. Do we talk about our amazing 600 heritage buildings, our being the historic heart of Canada, our waters and our water lifestyle? Our being the fresh water sailing capital of the WORLD? That boating is unsurpassed here? The same with canoeing, kayaking, or fishing? That we have a proud military history for 340 years? That we are 30 minutes away from the most southerly wilderness park in Canada? That the United Empire Loyalists chose to come here and start a new nation? That we have the oldest farmers' market in Canada? That we have a skating rink behind City Hall? That we are the first Capital of Canada, had the first Governor General, and Sir John A. himself, the Father of Confederation? **It is time we celebrated all these amazing things, not ignore them, and certainly not denigrate them.**

*We must engender pride in the citizenry.
*We must enlist the aid of everyone to "sell" the city.
*We have to brag -- and we have every right to brag.
*We have to chart a new course and overcome the fear of change.
*We need vision for the Kingston of tomorrow.
*We need to get on with the job.

# Chapter 5
# Vision

The city needs to attract business and new people. As mentioned, we have every attribute and asset to be a boom town -- every single one. What is wrong with the city?

**And the honest answer is...... absolutely nothing. But ---**

*We need clear vision for the city.
*We need a champion to lead the way.
*We need a collective effort to move toward a goal.
*We need to communicate our strengths to the outside world and more importantly, to ourselves.
*We need a plan.

Not having a plan is a plan to fail.

A vision statement is the guiding image of success. It is a blueprint for what the City wants to become. It is our preferred future. It must enunciate our communities' goals, guide the actions of all involved, reflect our knowledge and philosophy and define how our city government will operate in the future.
**It must inspire.
The city will never be greater than the vision that guides it.**

What do we want to be?
A city that embraces and works hand in hand with its major employers.
A city that leads the way in social services, innovation and education.
Where every child has a bright future.
Where we welcome new people and new ideas.
Where businesses seek out what we have to offer.
Where we proudly celebrate our 19$^{th}$ Century past and seek to share it with the world but boldly build alongside it for the 21$^{st}$ Century.
Where we reward innovation and entrepreneurship.
Where we stop selling ourselves short and believe in our possibilities.
Where green is an objective, not just a colour.
Where we foster community pride.
Where we retain our skilled graduates.
Where we attract the best scholastic, military and medical minds.
Where we break down silos and work to a single goal of excellence.
Where negativity is replaced by optimism.

# Chapter 6
# An Economic Development Discussion

We have already seen that we have an enviable list of assets to attract businesses and the desired workforce to staff them.
We have already seen that we have all the physical attributes to succeed.

Towns and cities all across North America are struggling to find an amenity that people want to experience. Some have one or two such amenities. The lucky ones have become boom towns attracting the coveted technology-based workers and, as a result, are attracting businesses. Boomtowns share many attributes -- waterfront, water lifestyle, institutes of higher learning, heritage, ambiance and authenticity, music, restaurants, entertainment, arts and culture, farmers' markets, architecture, health care, safe neighbourhoods, and access to major cities when needed.
SOUND FAMILIAR?

Economic Development revenues derive from several sources:
a. Tourism.
b. New residents -- workers, career changers and retirees
c. New businesses -- large, medium and small, entrepreneurs
d. Visiting business people -- Donald Gordon Centre, Queen's Executive MBA, Queen's parents, Alumni

Each are important targets and must be addressed.

## EDS & MEDS -- An Opportunity

If a city loses its industries and other industries are taken over by foreign investors, who then supplies the engine for economic growth in the community?
The answer is institutions with deep roots in the community, large numbers of employees that are not subject to takeover.
In other words, EDS & MEDS -- universities and hospitals. The biggest players in Federal grants are Medical research institutes and universities, their medical schools and teaching hospitals. Boston has followed this route with 48 universities, medical research facilities, top-ranked medical centres, and technology transfer institutions in computing, information technology, medical devices, biotechnology and genetics.

According to Richard Florida, the talent class of workers attracted to EDS & MEDS are looking for interesting streetscapes, city life with cafes and restaurants, a thriving music scene, art, literature, theatre, design, an outdoor lifestyle, and authenticity...Exactly what Kingston has to offer! Universities and medical centres once considered auxiliary players are now "inside actors and real players".

**Kingston is uniquely equipped to move in this direction.**

## THE ECONOMIC DEVELOPMENT MODEL

Every time out, Kingston can put together a pitch team unequaled in talent, experience, intellectual property, and scope. Let's envision a team that would make a pitch to a large pharmaceutical company looking to expand. The pitch team would comprise:

A. Queen's University Head of Medical Research
B. CEO of KGH
C. The Mayor, with guarantees to streamline processes and offering tax breaks
(this is how Mel Lastman built North York into the fastest growing city in Canada)
D. The President of a large corporation in Kingston to speak to the social advantages of a business residing in Kingston
E. The head of the Cancer Research Institute of Canada to speak to the brain trust available
F. Kedco to speak to lifestyle advantages of the city outdoors (i.e., sports for children)
G. Head of Parteq to speak to the available talent pool
H. Retired head of a major company in the related field

The group asks for the order.

For each pitch, the Dream Team changes to fit the prospect, the situation, and the need. Professors from RMC, military leaders and retired military leaders are a huge intellectual property. The city needs to take a leadership role in this process at the highest level.

Structure a working committee.
Select and recruit appropriate and best dream teams.
Select a champion for each. (This is where a military leader could prove invaluable: they know how to get things done!)
The Committee develops a strategy for each pitch.

Ensure that processes and infrastructures are in place to facilitate the startup.
Market each successful addition and merchandise to the appropriate cluster.

## The Albany Example

The author explained the above scenario to Dr. Karen Hitchcock, the then Principal of Queen's University. She advised that she had employed a similar technique in Albany, New York while Principal of the University there. She assembled a team of corporate CEOs to discuss economic development for the city. The process took several months, and the team identified three major business targets based on knowledge, research and contacts.

One of the targets was IBM. She contacted the CEO of IBM and requested a meeting with the person in charge of selecting sites for future expansion. The IBM official flew to Albany and met with the group, explaining in detail the requirements for consideration. The individual Albany companies each assigned a full time employee to the task. After a year, Dr. Hitchcock contacted the IBM official and he and his team travelled to Albany for the "pitch". IBM spent millions on a new facility in Albany. Dr. Hitchcock said that the Kingston example above was using the same technique, but substituting other CEOs for the corporate heads. She endorsed the idea completely.

In addition to all the amenities listed in the previous chapters, Kingston's location on the 401 affords easy access to Toronto, Montreal, Ottawa and upstate New York. Queen's University ranks #8 among Canadian universities for research funding, and has received over $250,000,000 in the last five years. Parteq Innovations is the #1-ranked technology transfer company in Canada. The Royal Military College is known for its expertise in fuel cells and defense-related innovations such as bioremediation. And St. Lawrence College is a leader in alternate energy studies.

\*\*\*

## A Matter of Attitude

Let me quote from the Elliot Lake Office of Economic Development:

"The City's Economic Development office operates as a key facilitator in the process of economic diversification in partnership with the City, Council, community business leaders and community minded residents. Staff are flexible and open to discussions about business ideas and economic development from both residents and interested business leaders from outside the community; in fact our office's role is to facilitate the process involved in taking ideas to reality. We're here to listen, then point you in the right direction or to get involved. All of this is supported by a forward-thinking Mayor and Council and the community partner organizations who can get behind economic development projects to move our economy forward. We are only a phone call away, or drop by City Hall to get things started."

How amazingly refreshing.

\*\*\*

Secondly, let me quote from the Mississauga ED plan. It is precise, well-defined and highly actionable. They know exactly what they want.

Goal: The city is committed to growth; it is a city that values strong global business, fostering a prosperous and sustainable economy that attracts and grows talent.

The city is a business magnet and will target opportunities in high growth sectors, ensuring a supportive business environment, and will provide a compelling brand to attract business investment and jobs.

We will develop local assets to create a high quality urban environment and cultural centre.

Drive innovation and economic impact.

Leverage our post secondary institutions, centres of excellence and research institutions.

Strengthen the relationship with business and education.

Develop a clean tech initiative.

Capitalize on the growth potential of bioinformatics.

Build a cohesive life sciences community by sustaining an on-going dialogue among leaders in academia, industry and healthcare.

A clear and well-defined and targeted plan!

# Key points from Chapter 6

Kingston has all the physical elements to succeed in economic development.

It is not a question of what is wrong with Kingston, but rather what is wrong <u>within</u> Kingston.

The city is not attracting businesses.

We are not using the intellectual capital of the city's population -- a major opportunity for the city.

We need a vision, we need a champion.

The City, Queen's University, Royal Military College, St. Lawrence College and Kingston General Hospital must all engage in the Economic Development process.


Opportunity:

*There is a huge opportunity to enlist the intellectual capital and natural assets of Kingston for sustainable economic development.

*Define where we are going with a clear, well defined economic plan.

*EDS & MEDS represent a unique opportunity for growth given our already superb resources in this area.


*"Ability is of little account without opportunity."*

# Section 2
# History and Heritage

# Chapter 7
# The Historic Heart of Canada

**History and Heritage.** Kingston is one of only four cities in Canada that has significant 19th Century buildings and the only one west of Quebec... A unique and important fact.

Long before the French explorers arrived in the region, Cataraqui was a gathering place for First Nations people, and Belle Island just off the inner harbour, was a First Nations burial ground and a place of great religious significance.

Noted Queen's historian Arthur Lower wrote, "History is in some ways to see the past as vital and living. History is an attempt to see backwards along the path we have come to perhaps glean some inkling of the path down which we are going. As a Canadian city, Kingston is unique for the structural materials of which it is constructed. **Much of Kingston built itself out of itself -- small wonder it is called The Limestone City."**

It was this same location that attracted the United Empire Loyalists, who came here to build a new nation based on British values, Parliamentary government, and Anglicanism. And, of course, they stayed to build the magnificent stone mansions and churches that still grace our city to this day.

It was our strategic location that prompted the construction of Fort Frontenac and later Fort Henry, from enemy encroachment -- a proud military history that remains very much with us.

Kingston is rich in history. The ten-block downtown area boasts 600 heritage buildings from the mid-1800's, not subjected to the bulldozer craze of the 50's and 60's when many Canadian cities lost their heritage. Not roped off from public view, but rather tangible reminders of more than three centuries of life.

Historian Alvin Armstrong wrote, "It is difficult to ignore the past in Kingston. The architecture remains, including both the magnificent and the mundane. The elegant City Hall, a legacy of the triumphant and exuberant Kingston of the 1840's, dominates its waterfront a few hundred yards from the partially-excavated foundation of Fort Frontenac, built in 1673."

Imagine, if you will, the incredible cast of characters who strode our streets: Champlain, Count Frontenac, Sieur de La Salle, Molly and Joseph Brant, John Stuart, Bishop Macdonnell, Lord Sydenham, founding families of the UEL and Sir John A. Macdonald.

Kingston is variously referred to as The Historic Heart of Canada, the Limestone City, the City of Education with Queen's University, the Royal Military College and St. Lawrence College, a boat-building city, a military city, a fort city, a city of magnificent architecture, the cradle of hockey, and the Fresh Water Capital of the World. These valuable assets represent a gold mine of opportunity for the city and its people.

Gettysburg, Virginia celebrates a three-day battle of the Civil War, and makes upwards of $95 million a year. Old Albuquerque promotes Old Town and makes millions in the process with just a handful of old buildings and one old church. Williamsburg, Virginia is one of the most popular tourist attractions in America and it isn't even authentic. Kingston has 600 old buildings and 13 heritage churches -- all are not only authentic, but still uniquely in daily use.

**History sells**

As an aside, my video partner and I started a history vignette website in 2012 featuring 60-second stories of Kingston's history (www.HistoryMoments.ca). We received an email from Google/YouTube stating that in the first 90 days we received 1,000,000 viewings and they declared us the **fastest growing history website in the world.** **(See Chapter 12)**

**History sells. And Kingston history sells -- all over the world.**

# Key points from Chapter 7

**Kingston is the Historic Heart of Canada.**

**Kingston is only one of 4 cities in Canada with significant 19th Century history and heritage.**

**The waters of Kingston have shaped our history, our commerce and now our recreation.**

**An amazing cast of characters have written on the slate of our history.**

**There is enormous opportunity and wealth in marketing our heritage and history.**

Opportunities:

History and Heritage sell worldwide.
1,000,000 viewings in 90 days world-wide to see Kingston history.
Gettysburg, Williamsburg, Old Albuquerque make millions selling history with a fraction of what we have.
We are the Historic Heart of Canada.
Our amazing cast of characters deserve a museum and the museum will attract tourism dollars.

Shipbuilding is a story.
Ship war art is a story.
Architecture is a story.
Hockey is a story.
Sunken ship photos are a story.

# Chapter 8
# The King Street Experience

**4 kilometres, 180 years, 66 points of historic interest on one street.**

To travel along Kingston's King Street is to take a journey back in time. You will pass some of the finest 19th Century homes in Canada, commercial buildings, government buildings and many places of historical significance.

We begin the journey at Kingston City Hall built in 1844. The mayor, John Counter, wanted a municipal building befitting the Capital of Canada. (Note: Kingston was Canada's capital from 1841-1844 before it was moved to Montreal, then Ottawa for security reasons, as Kingston was too close to the United States.) The City Hall was designed by architect George Brown, with the cornerstone laid by Governor General Charles Metcalfe June 5, 1843. Cost of the building was 28,000 British pounds.

Immediately behind City Hall is Market Square (now called Springer Market Square). The square has occupied this space for over 200 years and was laid out in the official city plan in 1784. It has served as a market site since 1801 (Canada's oldest continuous farmers' market). The first market regulations were published in 1811. During the War of 1812, a small barracks (35 by 22 feet) was erected on the site under what is now the south wing of City Hall, with other military buildings in the area of the current west wing. Following the war, wooden sheds occupied the site and were known as the Shambles. For many years, the Shambles was the only place where it was legal to purchase meat. The fire of 1840 destroyed most of the Shambles.

Immediately across King Street, the large red brick building is the British Whig building that housed the oldest daily newspaper in Canada. The land was the original site of the first St. George's Church, built in 1792 and demolished in 1825. The Whig building was erected by publisher Edward Pense in 1895, and designed by architect Joseph Power. The building now houses city staff.

Across the road on the same side to the west is Customs House, built in 1856-57 for government services for the united Canada. Of interest, the stone was supplied by the penitentiary and quarried by convicts.

Immediately on your right is St. George's Cathedral, the founding church of the Anglican Diocese of Ontario. The congregation first met in 1785 at the Tete-du Pont at Fort Frontenac, then in a 32 by 40 foot wooden building erected where the British Whig building now stands. The church was founded by Reverend John Stuart. A plaque at the cathedral reads:

*"Who came to this province as a United Empire Loyalist and was known as the father of the Anglican Church of Canada. He founded the church and also the first school. He was chaplain of the garrison to the first Legislative Council for twenty-seven years and Rector of Kingston. Associated with Tyendinaga (Joseph Brant), he translated the Gospels and the Common Book Of Prayer into the Mohawk native tongue. Universally loved this intrepid herald of the Gospel fell asleep August 15,1811."*

Reverend Stuart was succeeded by his son, Archdeacon George Okill Stuart, who was responsible for the the construction of the new church. Total cost: 3,000 British pounds, half donated by King George IV. The first service was held in 1825. The church was declared a cathedral in 1862 with the formation of the Diocese of Ontario. (Note: Of the fifty-four founding members of the congregation, only one was a woman, Molly Brant, sister of First Nations Chief Joseph Brant, and a woman who played a key role in keeping the First Nations people on the side of the British during the American Revolution. It is remarkable to think that in the late 1700's and early 1800's, a woman played such a prominent role in the church. The fact that she was a native woman, one can only imagine what an amazing and important stature she held in the community.)

In 1792, John Graves Simcoe was sworn in as the Lt. Governor of Upper Canada on the steps of St. George's. The Stuarts, father and son, presided over the church for 77 years, 1785-1862. They are both buried in the Stuart grave in the old Protestant cemetery of St. Paul's Church, at Queen and Montreal Streets. It is considered the oldest Protestant cemetery in Canada.

Across the road from St. George's, the large grey building is Empire Life. Originally the Commercial Bank of Midland District, built 1853-54, and designed by William Hay. The building was sold to Empire Life in 1936.

Next to Empire Life at 225 King St. East is the Frontenac Club, now a B&B. Built for the Bank of Montreal in 1845, it became a Men's Club in 1906, with guests including Alexander Graham Bell, Carl Sandberg and Prime Minister Mackenzie King.

264 King St. East (on the other side of the road) is Gildersleeve House, built in 1825 by Henry Gildersleeve, a Great Lakes Captain and shipbuilder. He built the first steam-powered vessel, "the Frontenac", to ply the Great Lakes. Henry was also President of Kingston Marine Railway and director of the Gas Company. The home was owned by the family until 1900. One of Henry's sons became the Mayor of Kingston. (Note the boot scraper flanked by a pair of dolphins at the front curb, as well as a pair of hitching posts and a stepping stone for descending from a carriage.) The small stone house to the side is known as the Architect's House, and was built in 1909 for Architect Henry P. Smith.

Next door are 254-256 King St. East, built in 1889-90 for John Thompson by Architect William Coverdale.

244 King St. East, corner house, was designed by William Newlands for Dr. Leonard Clements, one of the founders of the Queen's Medical School, and built 1890-91.

240 King St. East was built in 1829 by Archdeacon Stuart for a relative, Dr. Murray. In 1830, the house was Mrs. Leach's Seminary, and in 1837 served as offices for Reverend William Herchmer and William Ferguson.

232 King St. East was built in 1812 by the Stuart family as a rental. Later known as Davis House (owner of the drydock).

220-222 King St. East, just down the road, is a 2-storey double house built in 1868 on land bought by John Neill in 1866.

224-226 King St. East was built in 1843 by John Watkins and Samuel Mucklestone, merchants.

Across the road (on the uneven-numbered side) and next to the Frontenac Club, is a home built in 1834 for John Solomon Cartwright and his wife, Sarah. John was a descendent of an original Loyalist family who had come to Kingston in 1784. He was a member of the Family Compact.

And 203 King St East, Knaresborough Cottage, was built in 1843 by Thomas Rogers from a design by John Power for Ann Macauley. Ann was the mother of the Honourable John Macauley. The home remained in the family until 1947.

212 King St. East (back on the even side) was built in 1843-44 on land owned by Edmund Boyle.

204 King St. East was built by Duncan St. Clair in 1851 for John Craig, who worked as a carpenter during the building of City Hall.

Adjacent to it, the small red brick house at 202 King St. East, was also built in 1841.

The house to the right (198) was built in 1853 for Robert Seller and rented to George H. Seller.

194 King St. East was built in 1838 for George Oliver -- one of the first houses on the street.

191 King St. East (across the road) was the home of Robert Cartwright and his wife, Harriet, built in 1833. Robert (twin to John Solomon) was the assistant minister of St. George's Church and a member of the Legislative Council of Upper Canada. Their son Richard became the Federal Minister of Finance, Trade and Commerce for the Liberal Party of Canada, and handled the party's financial matters for over 50 years. The home was sold to Sheriff William Ferguson in 1877. The stone and iron arrowhead fence is original to the home.

169 King St. East was built 1885 for banker Donald Fraser by architect William Newlands.

167-165 King St. East was designed by William Coverdale, and built in 1857-58 for Richard Cartwright. It was rented to Richard's brother, Conway.

161 King St. East, at the corner of Lower Union, was designed by architect John Power for his son-in-law, Noble Kent.

157 King St. East was built in 1882 from a design by Joseph Power. It was the home of Dr. Edward Horsey, and sold to the Federal Government in 1887.

156 King St. East (immediately across the road), known as Earl Place. Built for Collin Miller, son-in-law of Captain Hugh Earl of the Provincial Marine. (The Captain's wife was Anne Earl, daughter of Molly Brant and Sir William Johnson.) The house was later known as Montague House and, later still, sold to the Knights of Columbus. Note the last gas lamp in Kingston in front of the house. Gas lamps were installed in Kingston in 1847, one of the first cities in Canada to install gas lamps.

141 King St. East (just slightly west on the uneven side), now the Belvedere Hotel. Built in 1880 by architect Joseph Power for John Hinds. It was sold to Dr. Kenneth Fenwick in 1887.

138-132 King St. East (across the road) was a row of houses known as Washington Terrace. Built in 1875-76 for Byron Moffat Britton, a judge and mayor of Kingston. Architect Joseph Power & Son.

131 King St. East (back on the uneven-numbered side) was designed by William Coverdale and built for Noble Palmer, founder of the Kingston Spectator. Half of the home was occupied by Governor Charles Metcalfe in early 1843, while his predecessor Sir Charles Bagot lay dying at Alwington House. In 1851, the house became the Kingston Seminary for Young Ladies.

123-125 King St. East was built in 1875 by William Mudie and sold to his son John, a lawyer.

130 King St. East (across the road) was built in 1874 by architects Power and Son.

95 King St. East (on the next corner) is Hendry House, built in 1886 for James Hendry, a wholesale grocery supplier. The Whig called the home "probably the handsomest house in the city this year".

85 King St. East was known as The Kent House, and built in 1877 for Rybert Kent, proprietor of the British American Hotel. The house was designed by John Power and built of limestone. It was later known as Dalton House for owner John Dalton, who lived there from 1928-1962.

81 King St. East, Upper House. Built in 1841 for John Watkins, a hardware merchant. John Watkins donated the Watkins Wing at Kingston General Hospital. Enlarged in 1886 by William Newlands for Joseph Upper.

53 King St. East (at Maitland), Murney House. The land on which the house stands was part of the land granted to Captain Michael Grass, who led the Kingston contingent of the UEL in 1784. Part of the land was then sold to Captain William Murney in 1808. When Kingston was declared the Capital of Canada in 1841, the Federal Government bought a large section of the Murney land from the Captain's widow. Mrs. Murney retained the waterside property and built her home there. When the capital was moved in 1844, the land was no longer needed for a parliament building and was given to the City as a park, City Park. Murney House was sold to grocery

merchant Andrew McLean in 1855.

49 King St. East, Medical House, was built in 1879 for Edward Barker Pense (owner of the British Whig) by architect Joseph Power. Later known as the Bishop's Court. In 1950, the building became the Student Medical House Corporation.

45 King St. East was built in 1853 for Captain William Bowen, a steamship captain, by John Power. Sold to Charles Gildersleeve in 1867.

31 King St. East, Parkview House, was built in 1853 for Charles Gaskin, a merchant, by architect John Power. Located on part of the original Murney land which had been subdivided in 1840. Note that #7 & #9 Emily Street were built on land that was part of the coach house rear wing and servants' quarters for Parkview House.

City Park (across the road). The park was the first official city park in Canada. At the southeast corner is a statue of Sir John A. Macdonald, the first Prime Minister of Canada and the father of Confederation. Sir John grew up, lived, worked and is buried in Kingston. The statue was erected in 1895, four years after his death. At the back of the park is the Frontenac County Court House, built in 1855. The original court house built in 1796 stood at the corner of Clarence and King streets where Customs House now sits. The new Court House was severely damaged by fire in 1874, but rebuilt by William Newlands from the original plans. The Court House witnessed six public hangings from 1867 to 1949. The Court House reflects the design of City Hall.

Just west of the park is Kingston General Hospital. In 1813, a citizens' group met to discuss raising 1,000 pounds to build a hospital. The Provincial Government added 3,000 pounds. Although completed in 1835, the hospital did not open for three more years, as it could not afford equipment and furniture. The building was used as the site of the first Parliament in Canada.

Opposite KGH, you will find Macdonald Park, a gift to the city from the British Government when the land was no longer needed for defense purposes. The transfer was decreed in the Confederation Act of 1867. Note the park houses three historic buildings:

A. Murney Tower. In 1846, in response to the Oregon Crisis, the British Government decided to strengthen various Canadian sites and built four Martello Towers in Kingston. Murney Tower, now a museum, was considered the most sophisticated Martello Tower in North America.

The tower was originally named Murray Redoubt for Sir George Murray, but the name was changed to Murney Redoubt and, therefore, the odd and incorrect spelling of the name in the brick (Murnay).
B. The ornate bandstand by the water is Newlands Pavilion, designed and built by William Newlands in 1896. Note the roof pattern emulating the waves on the lake.
C. Richardson Bath House was a bequest in honour of Captain George Taylor Richardson to the children of Kingston. Captain Richardson was killed in action in WWI in 1916. His death was partly responsible for the introduction of the Memorial Cup. The Bath House opened in 1919.

(* Street numbers are now King St. West.)

165 King St. West was built in 1878 for William Downing, a partner in a brewery known as Downing, Wales and Jewell.

189 King St. West, Willow Cottage. Designed by architect William Coverdale, and built for the Reverend William Macaulay Herchmer.

Hales Cottages (a row of white houses), #311-317 King St. West. These were built in 1841-44 by Charles Hales as living quarters for federal government employees. The location is midway between parliament (KGH) and Alwington, official residence of the Governor General of Canada. It is said that the rubble from the construction of the cottages caused Lord Sydenham's horse to spook, throwing him. Sydenham died from his injuries and is buried under the knave of St. George's Cathedral.

440 King St. West (a large, yellow stucco home) is St. Helen's. Built in 1837 by Thomas Kirkpatrick on 12 acres of land on Lake Ontario. One of Kirkpatrick's sons, George Airey, became the Lieutenant-Governor of Upper Canada. Thomas was the first mayor of Kingston after it was incorporated as a town in 1838. Unfortunately, St. Helen's was outside the city limits and Kirkpatrick was forced to resign as mayor. Over the years, the home has been known as Mortonwood, Ringwood House and Ongwanada.

437 King St. West, Copsworth. Built in 1878 for James Craig, a wholesale merchant. Architect William Newlands (at the time working for Power & Son).

Up the road just before Kingston Penitentiary was the site of Alwington House, official residence of the Governor General of Canada when Kingston was the capital of Canada. (The street is now named Alwington Place.) Built in 1834 by Charles William Grant, son of David Alexander

Grant of the 84th Regiment and Marie Le Moyne Grant, Baroness of Longueuil whose family owned Lemoine Point. It was leased to the Federal Government. Despite the short stay of Kingston as the capital, two Governor Generals died in the house. There is a plaque on the grounds commemorating the location.

Kingston of Upper Canada Penitentiary was constructed in 1833-34 as the Provincial Penitentiary. The first inmates were housed there in 1835. Designated as a historic site in 1997, the prison was closed in 2013. Immediately across the road is the Warden's House, now the Prison Museum. Adjacent to the museum is the former Women's Prison (built in 1934 and de-commissioned in 2000).

Portsmouth Village (originally Hatter's Bay) is just down the hill from the prison. The land was granted to United Empire Loyalists in 1784. Construction of the prison in 1833 prompted rapid growth of the village. Officially incorporated in 1858, the village was annexed by the City of Kingston in 1952.

Adjacent to the prison is Portsmouth Harbour, site of the sailing venues for the 1976 Summer Olympics. The facility hosts several Canadian training regattas (CORK) each year. Kingston is recognized as The Fresh Water Sailing Capital of the World.

623 King St. West (opposite the harbour) is Portsmouth Town Hall, built in 1865 by architect William Coverdale. The hall is now headquarters for the St. John Ambulance. Over the years, the building has been used as a meeting hall, fire house and armory.

640 King St. West is now Peter's Drug Store. The original home was built in 1840, and served as the first post office for the village in 1856.

643 King West was built prior to the 1850's, and was a tavern from 1861-1865 operated by John Marks, and later a hotel operated by James Short.

658 King St. West is a small cottage built for Richard Logan in 1837. The property was sold to Richard Gibson, a keeper at the penitentiary around 1850, and the family lived here until the 1900's.

622 King St. West was originally owned by William Mudie, reeve of the village.

670 King St. West, the Portsmouth Orange Hall, was built in 1878.

678 King St. West was built in 1849 for John Hilliard. Sold to Thomas McCarthy in 1862, it became a grocery store and tavern.

685 King St. West, Sunshine Cottage, built in 1889.

711 King St. West was built in 1855 as a Methodist Church, "Holiness Church". Built on land purchased by Robert Jackson from the estate of Lt. Colonel C.C. Foster.

The Church of the Good Thief (up the hill) was built in 1892 by architect Joseph Connolly. The stone was quarried by convict labour. The church is named for Dismas, the Good Thief. Dismas, one of the convicts crucified with Jesus, prayed for a place in heaven and Jesus replied, "Thou shalt be with me in paradise." Dismas is the patron saint of those condemned to die. A portion of his cross is preserved in the Chapel of Relics, Santa Croce Geruselmme in Rome. There are numerous Dismas chapels in prisons throughout the world. However, the Portsmouth church is the only church dedicated to Dismas outside of prison walls. The presbytery at 747 King West was built for the priest of the church in 1895. The church was closed in 2014.

Your journey through time has come to an end. I hope you enjoyed the tour and the wonderful old heritage buildings and homes of King Street.

# Key points from Chapter 8

Kingston's King Street is unique in that in just 4 kilometres there are 66 points of historic significance, from stately limestone mansions to commercial buildings all still in daily use. How lucky we are to have them in our midst.

The Kingston downtown core has over 600 heritage buildings and represents a goldmine of tourism opportunities. Every building has a story to tell. History and heritage is one of the main draws for tourism worldwide, and Kingston is only one of four cities in all of Canada with a significant 19th Century history and the only one west of Quebec.

Opportunities:
King Street is a tourism opportunity.
The church tour is a tourism opportunity.
An architecture tour is a tourism opportunity.

*"Unfortunately, there seems to be more opportunities than abilities."*

# Chapter 9
# The Stories and Storeys of Store Street

Princess Street, formerly known as Store Street, represents the beginnings of Kingston's retail and social life. Fortunately, many of the buildings remain, still in daily use after more than one hundred years. Come with us as we explore some of the earliest merchants and their wares. As you walk along the thoroughfare, imagine women in their long dresses and matching hats, men in high starched collared shirts, the shopkeepers bustling about, and horse-drawn carriages and early motor cars dodging around each other on the busy street. And remember to glance up at the amazing and beautiful 19th Century architecture of the upper storeys, perhaps some of the finest examples of the period in all of Canada.

> "Kingston people hold the establishment in high favour, appreciating the sterling merits which are here evidenced."
>
> -- British Whig Anno Domini, 1909

The Commercial Mart, northeast corner Princess and Ontario Streets. Originally a house and a store (1820). Purchased by Charles Hale in 1837 and expanded with rounded corners and two stores and houses. Designed by George Brown. After many years as a market, the building became a piano factory, government warehouse and the S & R Department store. The building now houses offices and a restaurant.

#34 was the livery of R.E. Wilson. The firm had horses and boasted "careful drivers with up to the minute appointments".

Princess & King. L.W. Murphy grocery and provisions, "exporter of cheese to the old country." Established 1888.

#51 -- J. A. Wiseman Saddlery and Harness was established in 1906 and was located "just one block from City Hall".

#64-66 was home to John McGall, "tobacconist of rare merit", and featured a shoe shine parlor on the premises offering a morning shine to its patrons. Opened in 1903.

#68 -- Built in 1819 as a home for Patrick Smyth on land purchased from F.X. Rochleau. In 1893, the owner George McGowan had it redesigned as a store.

#70-72 -- Rochleau House, built in 1808. The date FXR 1808 is carved into the upper wall. Once served as Sir John A. Macdonald's law office. **Rochleau House is considered the oldest remaining house in Kingston.**

#73-75 -- The J.A. Hendry Grocery store, established in 1837. The local merchant for Redpath Sugar, E.B. Eddy paper products, Cow Brand products and Quaker Oats.

#77 -- Now Vandervoort Hardware, the building was constructed in 1820 by John Moore as a coffee house stop for stagecoaches travelling between Toronto and Montreal. By 1840, the building housed a military hospital. Up until 1868, the long wing at the back housed the Princess Street Grammar School. By 1888, Elliot Brothers occupied the space and offered plumbing, steam fitting, hardware, gas fitting, galvanized iron cornice work, copper work and tinsmithing.

#78 -- James Redden & Co. wholesale grocers. Established 1871.

#79 -- Opened in 1908, H.W. Newman Electric Co. offered all kinds of electric supplies, electric and gas lighting, installation of lighting and bells and electric motor repairs.

#81 -- Clark W. Wright Insurance, established 1904, originally built between 1875-1895. Mr. Clark was the Mayor of Kingston in 1895.

#84 -- Discerning buyers could find fur coats and hats at Campbell Bros., the exclusive agent for Buckley's Derbies of London, England. The firm carried what they described as "old Country stiff and soft hats".

#85 -- Mrs.Tolbert's hat shop until 1853.

#86 was the Kingston home of Toronto's Wm. Davies Co. Ltd., the largest meat packer in the Dominion. The operation was housed in this brick building from 1903.

#88-90 -- Angrove Brothers sporting goods: fishing, yachting, hunting and camping, as well as Ford and Oldsmobile bicycles. Established 1897.

#89-91 -- Taylor and Hamilton tinsmiths, plumbers and steam fitters. Housed here in 1903, the tradesmen produced cutlery, graniteware, copperware and stoves. "Kingston people hold the establishment in high favour, appreciating immediately the sterling merits which are here evidenced."

#92 -- Henderson's photo shop featured platinum and carbon finished pictures.

#93 -- Thomas McCauley, bookstore and general stationery.

Corner Wellington and Princess. James Johnston footwear: boots, rubbers, suitcases, and trunks. Featured "Dr. Reed Cushion shoes and Dr. Vernon Cushion Sole shoes".

#101 -- Built in 1841 by Captain George Smith and let to grocer Abraham Foster.

#106 -- Stacey & Stacey dry goods. The store moved to 118-129 after 22 years at the original location. Featured millinery, ladies wear and linens. "The result is that the trade is amongst the most particular ladies of the city." Mr. Stacey was President of the Kingston Retail Merchants Association.

#107 -- John McKay. "From trapper to wearer, no middle man to reap his share of the profit." Featured the latest fashion ideas for the tourist and transient trade.

#112 -- Dwyer Brothers men's furnishings, established 1896. Hats, caps, ready-made clothing. "Superior line from Keystone Hosiery Co."

#116 -- Lockett Shoe Company, 1881. Started as Haines & Lockett in this two-storey stone building. Business was so brisk it required "seven assistants to handle the transactions, and the house has a reputation of courteous service which is rendered to the patrons." The business featured Regal and Slater shoes for men, and Dorothy Dodd and Empress shoes for ladies.

#119-121 -- Erected 1852 and leased to Vincent and John Ockley, merchants and grocers. Store was still there in 1889.

#123-129 -- Built in 1854.

#122 -- Home to Newman & Shaw, "The Always Busy Store". Featured dry goods, whiteware and ready-to-wear garments. "One of the most popular places in Kingston for ladies to resort to in doing their shopping."

#124 -- L.T. Best Dry Hoods. Exclusive agent for Eastman Kodak in Kingston. Established 1874.

#125 -- Founded in 1849 by Charles Heath and sold to Dr. A.P. Chown, druggist, in 1889. "Speciality sick room supplies."

#128 -- George Mills & Co., established 1879. Kingston's "Famous Fur Store", it boasted that it was the largest furrier between Toronto and Montreal and specialized in Hawes hats. "The show windows are always dressed in the most attractive style, and at night they are ablaze with electric light."

#132-134 -- Crumley Brothers dry goods store opened in 1889, and featured "windows dressed with the latest importations in fashion". The store was the exclusive agent for ready-to-wear Crescent brand clothes.

#141 -- R. Uglow & Company, 1862, sold books and stationery.

#143 -- The Rudd Harness Corp., makers and sellers of quality leather harnesses, trunks and suitcases.

#155 -- Crawford and Walsh tailors. "It behooves us to take care in the selection of a tailor who is to make or mar other men's impression of us."

#157-159 -- The Standard Bank of Canada had 67 branches in Canada and was located at Princess and Bagot Streets. The building featured ornamental carvings in the stones.

#158 -- Beginning in 1869, M. Coates occupied this location and offered jewellery, optical goods, diamonds, watches, clocks and sterling silver.

#165-167 -- James Powell and family owned the building from 1840 to the 1880's. When fire raged up Princess in 1876, the building was saved from destruction by blowing up a small brick house to the west.

#166 -- A.J. Rees fruit "imported and domestic".

#168 -- T.R Carnovsky Bakery and confectionery, established 1849. The store was described as "scrupulously neat and clean" and featured a telephone, #111.

#170-172 -- John Laidlaw & Son, established 1884 as a "high class" staple and fancy goods store. "The very latest caprice of fashion and the newest and daintiest novelties in ladies wear are found here as soon as they are evolved by the originators of the fashion." The store was the sole agent for Butterick patterns in Kingston for 20 years.

#171 -- Henry Skinners National Drug and Chemical Company, established in 1848. The large building carried through to Queen Street. Capital stock was estimated at $6,000,000.

#173-175 -- Arthur K. Routley, a first class cigar and tobacco shop, boasted "everything for the devotee of the fragrant weed" including briar, meershaum and clay pipes.

#174 -- James Redden & Co. wholesale and retail groceries, established 1871. Sold coffee and imported teas from Ceylon.

#180 -- Home of the Montreal Stock Company selling silks, satins and dress materials. Established in 1894.

#181-183 -- W. B. Dalton & Sons, established 1877 as Dalton & Strange; the name was changed in 1904. Sold shelf and heavy hardware, farm implements, tools, cutlery, brass, tin, granite, iron and sorting goods. Required 14 assistants and 2 travelling salesmen.

#182 -- J. Crawford Grocery, established 1889. "High class groceries and general provisions. Every possible modern invention in the way of labour saving devices, such as the patented meat cutter."

#184 -- Thomas Peters & Co. confectionery and refreshment parlor, established 1904. "Has a reputation all over the city for his delicious candies, as well as ice cream and beverages."

#187 -- The Midland Shoe Company, established in 1905, offered a full line of leading Canadian and American boots, including Maple Leaf Brand Boots.

#189 -- S. J. Horsey stoves and hardware agent for Gurney-Tillen Souvenir stoves, since 1851.

#191 -- Warwick Brothers, "My Valet Laundry" dyeing and cleaning. Features the "newest ideas in men's neckwear".

Corner Princess and Montreal Streets. Sold household hardware, tools, farm implement, oils, varnish and Elephant brand paint.

#202 -- W.J. Baker tobacconist, known for their special blends, including "Queen's Blend and Baker's Cut Plug". Established in 1887, the second floor housed a billiards parlor.

#204 -- The P.J. McLaughlin Bakery and Confectionery, founded in 1879, featured an ice cream parlor.

#205-207 -- The Windsor Hotel with 40 guest rooms was opened by B.M. Britton. The hotel was purchased in 1901 by J. McCue. "Attractively arranged, simple rooms for the use of commercial men. A dining room that is the model of neatness."

#214-216 -- Home of the Grand Hotel, one of the most modern hotels in Kingston, and conveniently located in the Opera House Block.

#217 -- The D.J. Dawson music store, opened in 1907, sold pianos, organs, musical instruments. Exclusive agents for Willis pianos and Knabe pianos, and the new Williams Sewing Machine.

#219 -- M.J. Dolan Harness and Saddlery founded in 1846. Rebuilt in 1877.

#224 -- C.H. Boyes photography and portraiture shop.

#226 -- W.J. Keeley Opticians and Jewellers offered fine silver and plated ware.

#228 -- Pearsall's Millinery, "patronized by many of the best ladies in Kingston". Established 1903, featured hats, ribbons, feathers, plumes, velvets, laces, silks, satins. It employed 13 milliners.

#229-237 -- The T.F. Harrison Co. sold and manufactured everything in the way of upholstered furniture and also sold carpets, linoleum and draperies.

#230 -- R.J. Reid offered a full line of furniture throughout its 18,000 square feet store. Mr. Reid was one of the first graduates of the Rochester Embalming College.

#232 -- Originally The Bijou Theatre, the T.G. Brown store sold music and art featuring fine art collections, landscapes, water colours, in addition to Heintzman and Wormwith pianos.

#236 -- Wood Brothers sold jewellery and fine watches, as well as the "Thermos Bottle, which has become such a deservedly popular commodity". Opened 1887.

#238 -- J.B. Quellette Tailors featured worsted, tweeds, cheviots and broadcloth.

#240 -- Kenney & Doyle Butcher Shop, featuring cooked and pickled fish.

#242-244 -- Founded in 1891, the J.T. Lochhead Photography Studio was located at 262 Princess for 18 years before moving to this location in 1902.

Princess and Sydenham. The Kingston Laundry Company was formed in 1902, and boasted "special attention to ladies apparel".

#252-256 -- James Reid established the Furniture Factory in 1854. In 1928, he purchased the Orpheum Theatre next door for casket production, which was later converted to a funeral parlor.

#260 -- McDermott Brothers, purveyors of music, instruments and stationery, known for its Foreign and American Magazines. Opened in 1901.

#266-268 -- The E. Beaupre & Company sold aerated water, liquors, Imperial & Dominion wines and "special Belfast Ginger Ale".

#272 -- Housed A. Arthurs Bakery and Confectionery. Mr. Arthurs worked with Gardeners Biscuits for 20 years before starting his own business in 1906. His cakes and breads were known "as both wholesome and toothsome".

#276 -- D. J. Garbutt Locksmith, established 1893.

Corner Princess and Montreal Streets. J.Y. Parkhill, established 1869, featured wholesale groceries, eggs, and "fancy creamery butter". The building was the former Oddfellows Hall.

#286 -- A.E Herod Shoe Store, "home of a famous Goodyear welt machine...made to order shoes for people who are fastidious about the style and fit of their shoes".

#287 -- James Stratford, taxidermist, noted for his work with birds, fish and deer heads.

#288 -- The H.F. Price Confectionery and Ice Cream Parlor, opened in 1903 and famous for its "delicious summer drinks".

#290 -- McIlquham's Livery, established 1889 had 28 horses and "careful drivers", and featured light livery, hacks, coupes and runabouts.

#297 -- G. Ainslee, butcher. Connected by phone #153. "The honourable business methods of Mr. Ainslee have been largely responsible for the large and high class trade."

Princess & Clergy Streets. The Kingston Granite and Marble Works, 1899. The company produced monuments for Lord Sydenham, Sir George Kirkpatrick, and The Honourable Alex Campbell.

The Grimason Hotel at Princess & Clergy offered accommodation heated by steam and lighted by electric and gas fixtures. The hotel had 24 rooms.

Also on Princess between Clergy and Barrie was the store of R.J. Carson, one of the most prominent wholesale grocery houses in the city, selling dried fruit, teas and "foreign groceries". Housed businesses from 1840's.

#312-314 -- Sold in 1852 to John Kelly, a grocer who offered spirits, provisions, pork, butter, flour and grain. The main building fronting on Princess was a private residence until after 1900, when it became a post office and "first class drugstore".

#320-322 -- Built in 1841. Queen's College held classes here between 1842-1844. It was used as a school until 1847.

#324-332 -- Sir Richard Bonnycastle, a Lieutenant Colonel in the Royal Engineers, lived here until his death in 1847. He was partly responsible for the construction of Fort Henry in 1832, as well as the Martello Towers in 1846.

#335 -- Louis Abramson, Gentlemen's Wardrobe & General Furnishings, established 1895. His success was attributed to "his fair and square methods".

#338-344 -- Sir John A. Macdonald sold this small house to Henry Grimason, who converted it to a stop for farmers at the end of market day. By 1900 it was known as The Farmers' Royal Exchange.

#338 -- In 1906, N. Nolan established a fancy groceries, tea and coffee shop here. Phone #720.

#341-343 -- Founded in 1850, Daniel Couper purchased this brick building in 1886, selling staples and groceries, convenience foods in glass and tin, table delicacies, flour and feed. Sales were reported at $40,000 annually. Daniel Couper became Mayor in 1909.

#351 -- McCandless Jewellery sold jewellery, cut glass, fine silver, plated ware, and a complete line of optical goods. Established in 1906.

#372 -- J. Mullen Monument Works, founded in 1905.

#390-392 housed James Laturney's Carriage and Wagon Shop from 1874.

#398 -- J. Turk sold furniture, stoves, antiques, Chippendale and Sheraton. Opened in 1889.

The Princess Theatre boasted 300 seats and featured "high class vaudeville and moving pictures...by keeping the performances thoroughly refined and entertaining, the best class of people have been attracted." Opened in 1907.

The Williamsville Hotel, established in 1873, was known as the farmers' hotel with a 10-horse stable at the rear. It also offered verandahs and a wide cement promenade in front.

# A SECOND THOUGHT ABOUT SECOND STOREYS

Kingston's beautiful and architecturally designed second storeys are not just confined to the second storeys of Princess Street. Here are a few other places to look up...

-from Ontario Street, walk up William Street

-from Ontario Street, walk up Earl Street

...there are wonderful examples on all. So take a walk and look up. You will be glad you did.

**Opportunities**:

**There are 98 stores profiled from 1910, and every single one represents an opportunity to increase foot traffic in the core. And the amazing second storey architecture only adds to the enjoyment of a stroll along our main shopping thoroughfare. Store plaques and posters could sell their history while adding an element of class and a touch of the past. It adds to the ambiance and uniqueness of "Princess Street".**

# Chapter 10
# Kingston and The War of 1812

A leisurely cruise down the St. Lawrence River and through the stately mansions and cottages of The 1,000 Islands reveals numerous forts and fortifications, visual reminders that a war was fought here. A war that pitted neighbour against neighbour. The War of 1812 was a war that no one really wanted, and it is hard to tell if anyone really won although "Canada", Britain and the United States all claimed victory. Britain obviously underestimated its adversary and were never sure why the Americans declared war as the main grievance was settled before the first shot was fired. The American Militia thought that they were taking part in the second American Revolution against British interference, when in reality the war was a thinly disguised political land grab for territorial expansion. An issue that would continue to threaten Canada for another 55 years (until Canadian Confederation in 1867).

The "Canadians" fought to defend their families, homes and farms, and the natives fought to try and regain their lands appropriated by the Jefferson government. When the war ended thirty months later, everything was returned to the status quo except the native lands. The "Canadians" and the natives who fought so valiantly were not even included in the treaty negotiations. Britain claimed they had won the war as no territory was lost, the Americans would appear to have won the Treaty, and the natives lost everything. But the "Canadians" were left with an almost mythical and unifying belief that they had single-handedly and repeatedly repulsed a huge adversary at their door.

Prior to the declaration of war, British commanders desperate for sailors to fight the Napoleonic War raging in Europe, were boarding U.S. ships and pressing (shanghaiing) the sailors into the service of the Crown. Adding to this affront, British Orders in Council gave the Royal Navy the right to seize the cargo of any ship leaving a French port. By 1812, over 400 American ships had been seized, wreaking havoc with American commerce. In retaliation, the U.S government, unable to attack Britain across an ocean, turned north to Canada. **The "Canadians" found themselves in a war that had nothing to do with them.**

The War was fought primarily in the Niagara region of Upper Canada, where the most of the American immigrants lived. They didn't want war, showed little interest in it, and most had relatives on both sides of the border. In Atlantic Canada, the War was just a newspaper story and commerce continued back and forth across the border.

The war started out as a gentlemen's war, with officers cordially greeting each other. When news of the declaration of War reached Fort George, where British were entertaining their American counterparts, both sides agreed to finish their meals, then calmly went to their respective forts to prepare for war. And when British General Brock was killed at Queenston Heights, American officers joined in the mourning.

Seasons, weather and harvests determined much of the fighting; troops on both sides thought nothing of leaving to return home to harvest their crops. Both sides spoke the same language, making it hard to tell friend from foe. Former U.S. President James Madison thought it only "a matter of marching", as most of Canada was populated with former Americans who would undoubtedly join the cause. Not to mention that the U.S. had a population of 8,000,000, versus Canada with a meagre 300,000. But the so-called former Americans had been here for a generation, had farmed, had raised a family and they were not about to give that up or to see it plundered. So fight they did.

The War lasted thirty months, and by war standards, casualties were light. The British counted 1,600 dead, the U.S. 2,260. But people on both sides died horrible deaths from cannon fire Troops were ravaged by winters -- men slept on frozen ground without adequate protection -- and were marched through frozen rivers. At any point in time, it was reported that one-third of the soldiers on either side were sick. Women and children were burned out of their homes and farms. Many of the American officers were often promoted for longevity of service, rather than competency, holdovers from the Revolution thirty-six years earlier. On the British side, many of the officers were cast-offs from the Napoleonic War in Europe or had purchased their commissions.

Both militias were ill-equipped and ill-trained, and desertions and mutinies were common. Many Americans refused to cross the border and fight on foreign soil, as their new constitution specifically stated that the militia role was only to defend their nation, not to attack another. The regular troops, trained in the traditional stand up columns, were easy targets for the stealth of the native fighters. Sanitation was non-existent, supplies were scarce, and proper food was rarely available.

In the summer of 1812, three American armies sat ready to attack at Amherstburg, Queenston and Kingston.

You have to wonder in hindsight just how could a small bunch of transplanted Americans with divided loyalties repulse a much larger opponent? Three reasons: One, the British troops under the command of Sir Isaac Brock were far better prepared and well spread out at forts throughout Upper Canada. Second, as noted, the American military leadership was old and the militia untrained. And third, the British-Indian Alliance, for without the considerable help of the native population under the leadership of Shawnee Chief Tecumseh, much of the region would have been taken early in the war.

Former U.S. President Jefferson's policies had stripped the natives of their land, and the natives saw an alliance with the British as a way to get their lands back. **"Therefore, it was left to a cobbled-together, ragtag group of ex-Americans, British Regulars, Scots, Irish and natives to defeat an invasion of their lives and lifestyle."** (Pierre Berton, The War of 1812.)

The total loss of property was estimated to be one million dollars, at a time when a soldier's pay was 25 cents a day. Compensation was not paid for another twelve years..

In the aftermath, few "Canadians" wanted an American style of republic, especially when there was a perfectly good alternative already in place -- that of British rule, orderly, conservative and secure. As Pierre Berton wrote in his two-part book on the War of 1812, **"How ironic that the myth of this strange, half-forgotten, ill-understood, unwanted and inconclusive little war remains today still firmly entrenched in the Canadian psyche as our defining moment."**

## Kingston and the War of 1812

Although most of the battles took place in the Niagara peninsula, there were battles and raids in the Kingston area.

November 21, 1812 -- The Americans raid Gananoque and destroy a military depot.

February 22, 1813 -- The British forces, under the command of Lt. Colonel George Macdonnell, raid Ogdensburg, New York.

May 29, 1814 -- The British capture Oswego, N.Y. and destroy the depot.

Throughout the war, American Generals were very reluctant to attack the fortifications at Kingston. The city's strategic location was key to maintaining the supply lines for the British troops. With the construction and launch of the St. Lawrence, a 3-storey, 112-gun warship, the British were able to control the Great Lakes for the remainder of the war.

The first shots of the war of 1812 were fired in Gananoque.

The Treaty of Ghent prohibited warships on the St. Lawrence River, a condition that is still in effect to this day.

The war was the **first military engagement for the American Navy.**

From July 1812 to September 1814, the upper region of the St. Lawrence River played a strategic role in **approximately twenty military actions occurring on both sides of the river.** Towns on both sides saw action: Gananoque, Sacket's Harbor and Kingston. Two major battles were in the Chateauguay area (Chrysler Farm). Fort Henry was built in 1812 to protect the Naval Dockyards, the major shipbuilding centre for the war and Home to the Provincial Marine (1784-1813) and the Naval Dockyards (1813 to the 1830's). The Naval Dockyards at Kingston were key in countering actions from Sacket's Harbor, site of the American shipbuilding yard.

**The incident at Bath, November 1812.** The British corvette, "The Royal George", commanded by Commodore Earl, was intercepted off False Duck Island by a seven-ship fleet under the command of U.S. Commodore Chauncey. Under pursuit, the "Royal George" escaped through a gap between Amherst Island and the eastern tip of Prince Edward County into the Bay of Quinte. The chase resumed in light winds the following day.

When the "Royal George" arrived in Kingston Harbour, Chauncey came under heavy fire from the guns of Fort Henry and had to withdraw..

In the aftermath of the war, the Rideau Canal from Kingston to Ottawa was built to assure that supply lines could not be cut off in the St. Lawrence River. Settlements along the canal were populated with discharged soldiers who were given free land.

The "HMS Radcliff" was the last ship built in Kingston; it is preserved in Mallorytown.

Brockville is named after General Isaac Brock, commander of the British forces for the war, who was killed at Queenston Heights in 1812. Although dying early in the war, Brock (by boldly attacking Detroit and being ready for the war, training his men for battle, and making the Indian Alliance with Tecumseh) set the tone that the Canadian side could win against a much larger foe.

During the war, Brockville was attacked by a force of 200 U.S. regulars and militia from Morristown, under the command of Captain Benjamin Forsyth who came across the ice. The raiders released 53 American prisoners from the Brockville jail. This raid prompted a counter raid on Ogdensburg two weeks later.

Gananoque was used as a forwarding point of the supply line from Montreal to Kingston. A group of U.S. Regulars and militia attacked the town in September 1812, led by Captain Forsythe of the First U.S. Rifles. The attackers seized the stores, burned the government depot and withdrew.

Prescott -- The site of Fort Wellington and a shore battery by the river, this village played a key role in maintaining the British supply line from Montreal. The town also housed the military hospital and barrack. In February 1813, Lt. Colonel 'Red George' Macdonnell led a force of 480 British Regulars and militia across the frozen St. Lawrence and captured Ogdensburg, New York, ending U.S. military presence in the town for the remainder of the war.

Cornwall, also a vital link in the supply chain, played a pivotal role in the defense of Montreal. In November 1813, U.S. Major General Wilkinson left Sacket's Harbor with a force of 8,000 men, and made his way up the St. Lawrence River with the intent of storming Montreal and choking off British supplies, effectively ending the war. However, he was followed by a British corps of 480 men, Regulars, militia, Canadian Fencibles, French Canadian Voltageurs, Mohawk Indians, and Douglas County Militia under the command of Lt. Colonel Joseph Morrison. Morrison made a stand against 4,000 of the U.S. contingent at Chrysler's Farm. But with odds of 10-to-1, he forced the Americans from the field. Wilkinson, with the rest of his force, continued up the St. Lawrence to Cornwall, but the citizens had emptied the depot supplies. The American troops were ordered to abandon the planned attack on Montreal and withdraw from the field.

The Battle of Chateauguay, October 26, 1812. A force of 1,630 French Canadian militia and Mohawk Indians under the command of Charles Salaberry repulsed an American force of 2,600. This battle, along with that of Chrysler Farm, caused the Americans to abandon the St. Lawrence campaign.

Sacket's Harbor was headquarters of the U.S. Navy on the the Great Lakes, and home to thousands of shipwrights, sailors and soldiers gathered to build, launch and defend the fleet. **One-third of the U.S army and one-quarter of the U.S. Navy were stationed here during the War.**

Ogdensburg, New York. When the war broke out, the Governor of New York, Daniel Tompkins, appointed Jacob Brown, a well-known smuggler, as Brigadier-General of the Militia in the northern border area. Brown decided to set up Sacket's Harbor as the shipbuilding base and Ogdensburg as the staging area for the army to conduct raids into British territory. A new Fort was built at Ogdensburg, Fort Oswgatchie. Throughout the fall of 1812, work continued on the fort and gun placements. However, before the fort was finished, the British launched an invasion of the town, effectively bringing all plans to use Ogdensburg as a military base to a halt.

1807 -- The "USS Chesapeake" was fired on and boarded by the British war ship HMS Leopold of Norfolk, Virginia.

June 1812 -- U.S. President Madison declares war on Britain.

September 21 -- U.S. forces attack Gananoque.

February 6, 1813 -- U.S. raid Brockville.

February 22 -- British capture Ogdensburg, N.Y.

May 29 -- British attack Sacket's Harbor, but are driven off.

August 23 -- British burn Washington

September 12 -- Siege of Fort McHenry (Baltimore); Star Spangled Banner penned.

October 25 -- American forces repulsed at Chateauguay.

November 11 -- American forces defeated at Chrysler's Farm.

February 8, 1815 -- Peace.

March 1 -- General Prevost officially notified of peace.

Fortifications in the 1,000 Islands Built for The War of 1812

Blockhouse - Chimney Island; Salaberry Island; Watchpost - Illes de France Watchpost - Grenadier Island, refuge for deserters; Thousand Islands archipelago; Fort St. Joseph - St. Joseph Island, British Military post; Bridge Island Naval Base; Fort Henry - Kingston; Fort Wellington - Prescott.

Ships built at the Kingston Naval Base during the War of 1812 (known as the Shipbuilders' War):

"HMS St. Lawrence" 1814
"HMS Prince Regent" 1814
"HMS Princess Charlotte" 1814
"HMS Duke of Gloucester" 1814
"Sir George Prevost " schooner 1813
"HMS Lord Melville" schooner 1813
"Psyche" frigate 1814"
"Niagara" gunboat 1814
"Queenston" gunboat 1814
"Chrysler" gunboat 1814
"Kingston" gunboat 1814
"Canada" unfinished 1815
"Wolfe" unfinished
"Sir Isaac Brock" burned on stocks 1815

## Fort Henry

A visit to Kingston must include a tour or event at Fort Henry, the Citadel of Upper Canada and now a UNESCO-designated World Heritage Site. Strategically placed high on a hill overlooking the mouth of the St. Lawrence, the fort was a huge deterrent to American attack. In fact, the fort was never attacked, testament to its location and power and as such, it played a significant role in protecting the British supply lines and the British shipbuilding operations during the war.

The fort cost 70,000 British pounds to build. British troops left the fort in 1870, and the fort was then maintained by Canadian soldiers until 1891. The Fort was restored in 1936-38 as a living museum, officially opened by Prime Minister William Lyon MacKenzie King. Of note, the Fort was used during the Second World War to house German prisoners of war.

**Martello Towers**

Despite the existence of the world's longest undefended border, Great Britain felt compelled to reinforce the defenses of Canada in response to the Oregon Crisis. The settlers in Oregon were moving toward their Manifest Destiny, asserting claims to large parts of the Canadian west (54-40 or fight).

The defences at Kingston were fortified in 1844 by the building of four Martello Towers in 1842:

i) one at Point Frederick (adjacent to the Royal Military College, it has three storeys and is now a museum). Of note, one of the young Scottish stone masons was Alexander Mackenzie, later the second Prime Minister of Canada.

ii) one at Murney Point, originally named Murray Tower, it stands near the hospital.

iii) another in Kingston Harbour (Shoal Tower, the only tower completely surrounded by water and built to protect City Hall and the harbour).

iv) one on Cedar Island (built to protect the eastern approaches).

Cost of the towers was 51,000 British Pounds.

These small defensive "forts" were up to 40 feet tall and divided into two storeys, with a single heavy artillery piece mounted on a flat 360-degree rotating platform; a movable cone-shaped roof was added to the Kingston Towers to protect the structures from harsh winter weather. A few were surrounded by a moat for extra protection. The first floor was often divided into different rooms, with fireplaces built into the thick stone walls for cooking and heating. Each garrison was manned by one officer and 24 soldiers. A total of 16 Martello towers were built in Canada, of which 11 still survive.

**The Voltigeurs**

Founded in response to the War of 1812, despite the fact that Britain and France had been at war during the Anglo-French War of 1627 to 1629, the Second Anglo-French war 1666-1687, the War of the Grand Alliance, the Nine Years War 1688-1697, the Seven Years War 1756-1763, the American Revolution 1775-1783, and the Napoleonic War 1792 to 1815.

When Canada was attacked during the War of 1812, Quebec's French Canadien Voltigeurs stood side-by-side with their English Canadian counterparts and fought with distinction. They played a key role in Canada's defense, at a time, as noted above, when England and France were at war in Europe. Recognizing that war with the United States was inevitable, Lieutenant George Prevost, General and Governor of the Provinces of Upper and Lower Canada, New Brunswick, Nova Scotia and the Islands of Prince Edward and Cape Breton, increased the military presence in British North America. He also raised a provincial corps of Light Infantry known as the Canadien Voltigeurs, under the authority of the Militia of Lower Canada. The soldiers were raised and paid for by The Province of Lower Canada, and were not part of the regular British army.

Officers were selected from prominent families of Lower Canada: six Captains and 18 Lieutenants, each raising their own recruits -- 36 recruits for Captains and 16 for Lieutenants. In addition, in 1813, two volunteer companies of Frontier Light Infantry were recruited and attached to the Voltigeurs.

During the early months of the war, the Voltigeurs were assigned the task of forward defense of the Eastern Townships. Led by Major de Salaberry, they successfully repulsed an American attack of 6,000 soldiers commanded by General Dearborn.

The following autumn, the Americans planned to cut off the St. Lawrence by seizing Montreal. On October 25, Lieutenant Colonel de Salaberry with 200 Regulars, two companies of Voltigeurs, 250 militia, and supported by Colonel George Macdonnell with 300 Voltigeurs and 700 militia, stopped the attack of 4,000 American troops.

**All the defenders were Canadians, both English and French, with no participation by British troops.**

On November 9, three companies of Voltigeurs, part of an 8,900-man force under Lt. Colonel Morrison, stopped American advances from Sacket's Harbor who were going to attack Montreal. The Battle of Chrysler's Farm, as the battle is called, saw the American forces driven from the field, and their mission to attack Montreal was abandoned.

On March 24, 1815, the Voltigeurs were disbanded, having played a significant role in the defense of their country. The unit Les Voltigeurs de Quebec found action again as part of the 57th Battalion of the Canadian Expeditionary Force in WWI, and as part of the Canadian Active Force in WWII.

Note: Information primarily gleaned from Pierre Berton's two magnificent books on the War of 1812, "The Invasion of Canada", Penguin Books, 1980, and "Flames Across the Border", McClelland & Stewart, 1981.

# Key points from Chapter 10

The War of 1812 had significant impact on Kingston, especially in the building of warships.

The War of 1812 was known as The Shipbuilders' War.

The War provided Canadians with a common purpose and common belief in themselves.

The War is an important story that most Canadians do not know or understand. Its telling represents tourism dollars.

Remember that Gettysburg makes $95,000,000 a year promoting their 3-day battle. History sells, and War History sells even better.


Opportunities:

Shipbuilding role of Kingston display.

Photos of sunken ships exhibit.

War of 1812 movie.

War art museum re: ships built here.

"St. Lawrence" Warship Museum could be a huge tourism opportunity. And could be incorporated as a unique and historic gallery in the Marine Museum of the Great Lakes.


*"He who refuses to embrace an opportunity looses as surely as if he has failed."*

# Chapter 11
# Cast of Characters

1. **First Nations**
2. **Count Frontenac**
3. **Sieur de La Salle**
4. **Lord Sydenham**
5. **Bishop MacDonnell**
6. **The United Empire Loyalists**
7. **Reverend John Stuart**
8. **Molly Brant**
9. **William Coverdale**
10. **Sir John A. Macdonald**

**1. First Nations People welcome the first French to the region.**

Aboriginal people have occupied the Kingston region for over 10,000 years. By the 1600's, the south shore of the St. Lawrence River and Lake Ontario were populated by Iroquois from the Oneida, Cayuga and Seneca nations. The villages at the end of the St. Lawrence included Kention (Consecon), Gannelious (Hay Bay), and Toniata (Brown's Bay). In June 1671, Daniel d'Reay de Courelle, Governor of New France, left Montreal and headed down the St. Lawrence River to a point where it met Lake Ontario. He observed that this would be an ideal place for a fort. At the request of the Five Nations, the new Governor Louis de Baude de Frontenac et de Palau travelled to Cataraqui. The natives waiting there in the morning of July, 1673 witnessed the site of a flotilla of 120 canoes, two flat boats, and 400 men in glittering French uniforms sweep up the channel between Wolfe Island and the north shore, and come into the mouth of the Cataraqui River. The natives referred to Frontenac as the Great Ononthio. The natives saluted the Governor and paid their respects to him for receiving them. The natives showed Frontenac the bay large enough for 100 ships but sheltered from the winds.

The following morning, Frontenac met with the Five Nations leaders at a point that is believed to be approximately the foot of Earl Street. Back up the bay, Frontenac's men were hastily erecting palisades and digging trenches for Fort Frontenac.

## 2. Louis de Baude de Frontenac

We have Frontenac County, Frontenac School, the Frontenacs Hockey Club, and many more things named for the man. Who was this person? Governor, soldier, statesman, fighter and founder of Kingston.

In 1620, in the principality of Bearne, France, Louis de Baude de Frontenac was born to a family of distinction. His grandfather, Antoine de Baude Seigneur de Frontenac, had attained eminence as a councillor of state under Henri IV. Antoine's children were raised with the future Louis XIII. Frontenac's father was a colonel in the regiment of Navarre and Captain to the royal castle of T. Germaine-en-laye. His mother was the daughter of the King's Secretary of State. Louis XIII was his grandfather.

Louis entered the army at the early age of 15, and in 1635 served under the Prince of Orange in Holland and fought engagements in the Low Countries and Italy where he received many wounds. In 1643, at the age of just 23, he was promoted to the rank of colonel in the regiment of Normandy; three years later by valour and skill, he was made Marechal de Camp. In 1669, he was sent to Crete in command of the troops against the Turks, and won further military glory. His brilliant military reputation preceded him to New France (Canada).

With crisis in the administration of New France, Frontenac was appointed to the post of Governor and arrived in Quebec on September 12, 1662. At this point, the entire population of New France was only about 6,000 scattered over a vast area.

During his first term (1662-1682), he built Fort Frontenac at "Cataracouy" to control the Iroquois and establish trade relations throughout the area. It is reported that one of Frontenac's party described the bay at Cataracouy as "one of the most beautiful and agreeable harbours in the world".

Frontenac also facilitated communications with the west, initiated exploration of the Mississippi (previously discovered by Joliet and Marquette), and sent Cavalier de La Salle to the south, where he would claim and name all the country watered by the great river in the name of his King Louis XIV: Louisiana.

Although intelligent, magnanimous and brave, Frontenac was also proud, imperious and argumentative, constantly quarrelling with other officials of the colony. The King ordered Frontenac back to France in 1682. The treacherous actions of Frontenac's successor as Governor created an Iroquois uprising and the Lachine massacre, which threatened the survival of the colony. Wisely, the King chose to ask his old friend Count Frontenac to return to New France, where he was hailed as the deliverer. The King is said to have told the Count, "I am sending you back to New France, where I am sure that you will serve me as well as you did before. I ask nothing more of you." Frontenac was called upon to fight both the Iroquois and the English, and his bravery and ability were certainly up to the task.

After d'Iberville's exploits in Hudson's Bay, Frontenac divided his forces into three corps and captured Cortar (Schenectady), Salmon Falls (New Hampshire, and Casco (Maryland). To avenge these attacks, the British sent a fleet of New England ships under the command of Sir William Phipps to attack Quebec. Phipps sent an envoy ashore demanding that the French surrender the Fort. Frontenac -- bold and fearless as always -- sent a defiant answer to Phipps: "Go tell your master that we shall answer him by the mouths of our guns." He completely repulsed the British fleet.

In 1696, Louis disregarded orders from Paris to evacuate the upper country, a move he believed would ruin the colony. Under his orders, d'Iberville quelled the Indians, razed Fort Pemquid in Acadia, captured St. John's, Newfoundland, and took possession of the entire Hudson's Bay territory. For his courage and prowess in the Indian wars, Frontenac received the Cross of St. Louis.

On one campaign, the old warrior (now 67) marched with his troops to the village of the Onondagas and back...a journey of one month each way.

After a brief illness, Louis de Baude de Frontenac died on November 28, 1698 at Chateau St. Louis, Quebec.

"He was fearless, resourceful and decisive, and triumphed as few men could have done over the difficulties and dangers of a most critical time. He had found a Canada weakened and attacked on all sides. He left it in peace, enlarged and respected. He was justly called the saver of the country."

References:

Catholic Encyclopedia, Count Frontenac by W. D. Le Sueur, Toronto, 1906. Count Frontenac in New France under Louis XIV by Francis Parkman, Boston, 1878.

## 3. Sieur de La Salle

Sieur Robert Cavalier de La Salle (1642-1687), famed French explorer, emigrated to Montreal in 1666. After being asked to oversee the construction of Fort Frontenac in 1674, he converted it from a crude wooden structure to one of stone. In 1677, he was awarded a monopoly of trade in the Mississippi Valley. On April 9, 1682, he took possession of the region watered by the Mississippi River and all its tributaries in the name of the King of France and named it Louisiana. In 1687, on a voyage from France, La Salle was killed in a mutiny by his own men.

## 4. Lord Sydenham

Charles Poulette Thompson was appointed Governor General of British North America in 1839 and was charged with the unification of Upper and Lower Canada into the Province of Canada. A task accomplished by The Union Act of 1840 with Lord Sydenham becoming the first Governor General of Canada. He established responsible government and municipal institutions, and summoned the First Parliament, which was convened July 2, 1841. Sydenham was described as "a handsome man of 40 with a gracious manner and fascinating smile". Due to failing health, Sydenham had tendered his resignation. However, on September 4th, 1841, while riding from Parliament (at KGH) to his official residence at Alwington, Sydenham's horse spooked at a pile of rubble next to the construction site of Hales Cottages (intended for parliamentary staff).

The Lord was thrown and dragged, succumbing to his injuries on September 18. Just weeks prior, he had attended St. George's Church for the first time and, after taking offense to the sermon delivered by Reverend Richard Cartwright, vowed never to set foot in the church again. He was buried under the knave, the only burial in the church. Sydenham was only 42 years old.

## 5. Bishop MacDonnell

1762-1840. Roman Catholic Bishop of Kingston in 1819. Appointed Vicar Apostolic of Upper Canada, and in Bishoptric in 1826. He was appointed to the Legislative Council, founded churches and schools throughout the region and, in 1846, founded Regiopolos College in Kingston, the first Catholic college west of Quebec. The original college is now part of Hotel Dieu Hospital.

## 6. The United Empire Loyalists

With the influx of Loyalist groups to Canada following the American Revolution, the history of Canada was vastly changed. Before 1784, much of Upper Canada was very sparsely populated by French traders. But the arrival of large numbers of British subjects led to the creation of two new provinces, Upper Canada and New Brunswick, joining Lower Canada (Quebec) and Nova Scotia. The Loyalists, fiercely loyal to the Crown, introduced British law, parliamentary government, British religion (Anglicanism), the British court system, and helped solidify British control over the northern half of the continent.

Most of the Loyalists were concentrated along the eastern end of the St. Lawrence River and Lake Ontario, from the Quebec border to the Bay of Quinte. The Cataraqui contingent, mostly from New York state, were under the command of Captain Michael Grass. The five Cataraqui settlements and eight St. Lawrence settlements comprised 1,568 men, 626 women, 1,492 children and 90 servants for a total of 3,776. They arrived in the area in 1784.

It can be said that the American Revolution created not just one, but two new countries.

## 7. The Reverend John Stuart

A plaque at St.George's Cathedral reads,

> *"Who came to this province as a United Empire Loyalist and was known as the father of the Anglican church in Canada. He founded the church and also the first school. He was chaplain of the garrison and to the Legislative Council for twenty seven years and was rector of Kingston. Associated with Tyendinaga (Joseph Brant) he translated the Gospels and the Book of Common Prayers into the Mohawk native tongue. Universally loved, this intrepid herald of the Gospel fell asleep August 15, 1811."*

John's son, Archdeacon George Okill Stuart, oversaw the construction of the current St. George's Church in 1825. The Stuarts, father and son, presided over the congregation of the church for 77 years (1785-1862). They are both buried in the old cemetery at St. Paul's. Church (Queen St.).

# 8. Molly Brant

Molly Brant was born in New York Province in 1736, a member of the Mohawk tribe. The Mohawks were a matriarchal society and, therefore, women chose the chief and handled economic matters, putting them in important political positions. After the death of Molly's father, her mother married Nickus Brant of the Turtle Clan. A master motivational speaker, Molly travelled with the Mohawk delegation to Philadelphia in 1754 to argue against fraudulent land claims.

Beginning in 1759, Molly became the common-law wife of Sir William Johnson, the British Superintendent of Indian Affairs (in New York). Molly bore Johnson eight children. A respected hostess, Molly interacted with ease among the colonists, placing herself in a sphere of influence in both white and Indian societies.

As tension mounted between Britain and the thirteen colonies in 1774, Sir William tried to keep the Iroquois loyal to the King, but he died of a heart attack. With the outbreak of war, Molly took up the cause, spying on behalf of the British, and offered shelter and provisions to Loyalists.

When the peace treaty ending the war was written in 1783, the First Nations people were left out and all their land south of the Great Lakes was confiscated by the American government.

The British rewarded Molly with a 116-acre plot of land in Kingston, and gave her a home, plus a yearly pension of 100 pounds. "In consideration of the early and uniform fidelity, attachment and zealous services rendered to His Majesty's Government by Mrs. Brant and her family." When St. George's Church was built at King and Johnson Streets in 1791, Molly was the only female member of the church founders -- a remarkable achievement for any woman in the time period, but unheard of for a native woman, attesting to her amazing presence and intellect.

Molly died on April 16, 1796, and is buried in the old cemetery at St. Paul's (Queen and Montreal Streets). Ian Wilson wrote of her, "Soldiers, statesmen, governors and generals wrote her praise. Her life was fraught with danger and uncertainty, but she survived this turmoil with dignity, honour and distinction."

# Interview with Molly Brant -- by Don Curtis

INTERVIEWER: Tonight we have a very special guest, and one to which we owe a debt of gratitude for her unfailing loyalty to the Crown during the harrowing days of the American Revolution. Author Ian Wilson wrote of her, "Soldiers, Statesmen, Governors and Generals wrote her praises. Her life was fraught with danger and uncertainty, but she survived the ordeal with dignity, honour and distinction." I speak, of course, of Molly Brant. Welcome Miss Brant. It is truly an honour to meet you.

MOLLY: Thank you so much for your kind words, and please call me Molly.

INT: Ok, Molly. Can you tell us about your early life?

M: I was born around 1736. I say around, because the Mohawk Nation doesn't record dates. I lived in the Mohawk Valley in the province of New York, and had a typical native childhood. That all changed when I went to work for Sir William Johnson, superintendent of India Affairs in New York. I was housekeeper and accountant for William's purchases and gifts to the Iroquois. William brought me into white society as his wife and we had eight wonderful children together.

INT: You mentioned 'white society'; is it true that you moved freely with both the white and Native groups in New York and, in fact, had considerable power?

M: I'm not sure that power is the right word. The Mohawk society is matriarchal and, as such, women looked after the economics of the tribe, and picked the leader. I was chosen leader of the Mohawk Clan Mothers. As to my role in white society, that was entirely William's doing. He insisted I be treated as an equal.

INT: If I may quote from a book about your life, you were "**highly respected by the Indians, as was her husband and she was versatile. She could dance around a fire with her Native friends and she could entertain the cream of white society graciously and properly in the grand rooms of Johnson Hall with their Chippendale furniture and fine china.**"

M: I find that a bit embarrassing. But, as I said, that was mostly to William's credit and reputation.

INT: Ok, let's get to the war. What was Sir William trying to accomplish?

M: William was a staunch Loyalist, and endeavoured to convince the Natives to side with Britain during the Revolutionary War. William realized that if the colonies won, the the Natives would lose all their land...Which, unfortunately, is exactly what happened in the long run. William died of a heart attack just prior to the outbreak of war. And I tried my best to carry on.

INT: You actually put yourself at great risk.

M: I suppose, but what are you going to do? I had Native rights to uphold, and William's work to carry on.

INT: Were you a spy?

M: Yes, in addition to constantly trying to keep the Iroquois nation on the British side of the war. I transported messages, helped Loyalists cross the border, hid people out at Johnson Hall, and helped many through the underground railway to safety in Canada. Even supplied guns and ammunition to my brother, Joseph, and his warriors.

INT: Any of those could have got you hung...

M: Yes, they could, but I was soon to flee to Canada.

INT: Can you explain the circumstances?

M: My brother, Joseph, along with 400 warriors plus a few white Loyalists, attacked and killed 800 patriots at the Battle of Oriskany, which ended all semblance of Native neutrality. In retaliation, General Washington sent eleven regiments to the area, and Joseph insisted that I take my children to Kingston. But even from there I was able to maintain contact with the tribe and help keep their loyalty.

Unfortunately, when the war ended in 1783, my people were not even part of the treaty. A line was drawn down the centre of the Great Lakes, and everything south of the line was taken by the Americans, and no Native lands were returned.

INT: For your efforts, the British Government provided you a home and land in Kingston, as well as a yearly pension of 100 pounds. Correct?

M: Correct. And I am eternally grateful, as I still had children to raise and no money.

INT: If I may read from the government decree, *"In consideration of her early and uniform fidelity, attachment and zealous services rendered to his Majesty's Government by Mrs. Brant and her family."* And that was not to be the end of your involvement.

M: In 1794, I was contacted by the American Government and offered a large amount of money to go America and negotiate with Native people regarding a potential Indian war in the Ohio Valley. I flatly refused. Joseph and I tried to get the Natives to negotiate and not go to war, as they were badly outnumbered, but the warriors attacked anyway and were soundly defeated at the Battle of the Fallen Timbers…

INT: Molly Brant died in 1796, and is buried along with several of her children in St.Paul's burial ground in Kingston. A glimpse of Molly Brant in Kingston was captured by a visitor to St. George's Anglican Church. *"In the church at Kingston we saw an Indian woman who sat in an honourable place among the British. She appeared very devout during Divine Service and very attentive to the service…When Indian embassies arrived, she was sent for, dined at Governor Simcoe's, was treated with respect by himself and his Lady. During the life of Sir William, she was attended with splendour and respect."*

## 9. William Coverdale

1801-1865, Kingston's Architect.

A perusal of the history of Kington's old buildings and mansions built between 1830 and 1865 reveals that many were designed by William Coverdale. Born in Yorkshire, England, he came to Canada with his family in 1832. He was employed by the Penitentiary and became Master Builder. As the architect of a major public building, his reputation soared and his services were in constant demand. He was free to take on private commissions as long as they didn't interfere with his work at the prison. In 1843, he designed and supervised the construction of Roselawn (now the Donald Gordon Centre) and added a new facade and Tower to St. George's Cathedral. When the Federal Government left town in 1844, many of the architects left as well, leaving Coverdale with little competition until 1850 when John Power came to Kingston.

Coverdale's work includes:

Sunnyside on Union St., designed for Mayor John Counter in 1845 and built in 1847. Originally called South Roode Cottage for Coverdale's wife, Hannah Roode.

The Earl street villas, between 1847-1850. Numbers 155, 162, 169, in addition to Rosemount at the corner of Earl and Sydenham (built for E.H. Hardy).

Two more villas in 1852: Elmhurst on Centre St. for Hugh Fraser, and Hillcroft on Union for Francis Manning.

A number of double houses were designed: 131-133 King St. East for Noble Palmer (1642); 165-167 King St. East for Richard Cartwright; Corbett House, on the southwest corner of Queen and Sydenham; the Mowat House; 230 and 228 Johnson (1852); Wellesley Terrace; and 270-286 on Johnson across from St. Mary's Cathedral.

Coverdale also built his own rental property at the corner of Bagot and West in 1856. That year, he was appointed architect for the Portsmouth Asylum for the Criminally Insane. Construction was not completed when William died in 1865. The buildings were finished by his son, William Miles Coverdale, later City Engineer.

## 10. Sir John A. Macdonald

> *"We are a great country, and shall become one of the greatest in the universe if we preserve it. We shall sink into insignificance and adversity if we suffer it to be broken."*

John's parents emigrated to Canada when John was five years old, choosing Kingston because they had relatives and contacts here. John attended both the Kingston Midland Grammar School and John Cruikshank School. He finished school at 15, and began study as a lawyer under the tutelage of Scottish expatriate and lawyer George MacKenzie. At 18, John opened a branch office in Napanee, and at 19 took over his ailing cousin's law practice for two years in Picton. When MacKenzie died of cholera in 1835, John decided to open his own practice, although he could not be called to the Bar until 21 (6 months away). First specializing in corporate law, John later switched to criminal law, a decision that would hone his public speaking skills.

John married his first cousin, Isabella Clark, in 1854; however, Isabella was permanently bedridden until her death in 1857. The couple had two sons, one of whom died in infancy. In 1867, John married Susan Agnes Bernard; their only child, a daughter, was born severely disabled.

Macdonald entered the world of politics in 1843, when he was elected City Alderman. The year after, he was elected to the legislature of the Province of Upper Canada to represent Kingston, and he would hold a number of political posts over the next two decades. He was nicknamed "Old Tomorrow" because of his penchant for putting off problems until conditions were favourable.

By 1864, John was working hard to organize the necessary legislation that would unite the colonies of Ontario, Quebec, Nova Scotia and New Brunswick. That September, Macdonald led the Canadian delegation at the Charlottetown Conference, but it took three years before an agreement was reached. In 1867, The British Parliament passed The British North America (BNA) Act, and on July 1st the Dominion of Canada was born. An election the following month swept Macdonald and his Conservative Party into power, and John became the first Prime Minister of Canada.

His vision was to enlarge and unify the entire country. This he did by purchasing Rupert's Land and the North West Territories from the Hudson's Bay Company for $300,000. He also founded the North West Mounted Police (later the Royal Canadian Mounted Police), in addition to creating the Provinces of Manitoba (1870), Prince Edward Island (1873), and British Columbia in 1871.

A promise to link the west with the east via a transcontinental railway led to accusations of bribery in 1873, and the Conservatives were defeated (John retained his seat). His government was, however, re-elected in 1878 on the strength of The National Policy, a plan to promote trade within the country by protecting it from industries of other nations. His dream of a transcontinental railway was finally achieved in 1885. That same year, he created the first National Park (in Banff).

On May 29, 1891, John suffered a severe stroke and died a week later on June 6 at Earnscliffe, his home in Ottawa. He was 76. Thousands paid their respects when he lay in state in the Senate Chamber, and thousands more watched his funeral train carrying him home to Kingston. He is buried along with his family in Kingston's Cataraqui Cemetery.

Sir John A. Macdonald led the country to maturity and security, dominating Canadian politics for 50 years (including 19 of them as Prime Minister). The Father of Confederation, John appears on the Canadian ten dollar bill.

On Macdonald's death, Sir Wilfred Laurier, leader of the Opposition, rose in the House with these words: *"The place of Sir John A. Macdonald in this country was so large and so absorbing it is almost impossible to conceive that the politics of this country, the fate of this country, will continue without him...His loss overwhelms us. For my part, I say with all truth, his loss overwhelms me and it overwhelms this Parliament, as if indeed one of the institutions of the land has given way...Sir John A. Macdonald now belongs to the ages, and it can be said with certainty that the career which has just been closed is one of the most remarkable careers of this country."*

## Career Highlights

He was instrumental in bringing all of the Hudson Bay land under Canadian control. He negotiated the entry of P.E.I. and British Columbia into the federation and helped establish the Province of Manitoba.

John's son, Hugh, sat briefly in the House of Commons with his father and later became Premier of Manitoba.

1847-38: Receiver General of the Province of Canada
1854-58, 1858-1862, 1864-1867: Attorney General of Canada West
1861-62, 1865-67: Militia Affairs
1867-1873: Justice and Attorney General
1878-1883: Minister of the Interior
1878-1887: Superintendent General of Indian Affairs
1889-1891: Minister of Railways and Canals

## Achievements

* Joint Premier of Canada with Etienne Paschal Tache (1856-57), and with Etienne Cartier (1857-1862).
* Co-leader of the Great Coalition with Cartier and George Brown (1863-1865) and with Cartier again (1865-67).
* 1868: negotiated the transfer of the whole of the Northwest Territories from Britain to Canada. The U.S. had offered Britain $10 million for the land.
* Created the Province of Manitoba (1870), brought B.C. (1871) and P.E.I. (1873) into Confederation.
* Acquired the land that became Saskatchewan and Alberta.
* Quelled the Red River Rebellion (1870) and the Northwest Rebellion (1885).

* Responsible for building the Canadian Pacific Railway (1871-1885) which brought all parts of Canada together.
* Established the National Policy (1879), encouraging the growth of Canadian industry.
* Founded the North West Mounted Police (later the Royal Canadian Mounted Police).
* Primary author and creator of the BNA Act.
* Created the first National Park in Banff, Alberta.
* First Prime Minister (1867-73) and later (1878-1891).
* Father of Confederation.
* Known for quick wit and a fiery temper.
* Nicknamed the Old Chieftain and Old Tomorrow.
* Only one of two Prime Ministers to die in office (John Thomson being the other).

## Sir John A. Macdonald and the Bottle

As Shakespeare wrote, "The evil that men do lives after them; the good is oft interred with their bones." So it may be with Sir John. Unfortunately, his considerable achievements in founding the nation are often overlooked in favour of focussing on his drinking. There is no doubt that John had a drinking problem, at times rendering him incapacitated and resulting in his absence from the work of the nation and the House for days at a time. John was a binge drinker and, therefore, not in a constant state of drunkenness. Starting in 1856 and lasting for some twenty years, John drank to excess in binges. Not to excuse the binges, but society at the time was a culture of taverns with 126 pubs in Kingston. John had faced a lot of adversity in his private life: his first wife was ill for 14 years, they had a baby die in infancy, and John's daughter by his second wife was severely disabled. And, of course, he faced enormous pressure in bringing the country together, not to mention the Pacific Scandal and the subsequent government defeat. Despite these transgressions, Sir John had a miraculous record of achievement.

## Famous Sir John A. Quotes

"Let us be English or let us be French, but above all let us be Canadian."

"A public man should have no resentments."

"Anybody may support me when I am right. What I want is a man who will support me when I am wrong."

"Give me better wood and I will make you a better cabinet."

"Harry, my boy, never write a letter if you can help it and never destroy one."

"I carried my musket in '37."

"I have no accord with the desire in some quarters that by any mode whatever there should be no attempt made to oppress the one language or to render it inferior to the other. I believe that would be impossible if it were tried and it would be foolish and wicked if it were possible."

"I got sick, not because of drink, but because I was forced to listen to the rantings of my Honourable opponent."

"I say that there is a deliberate conspiracy by force, by fraud, or by both to force Canada into the American Union."

"I would be willing personally to leave the whole country a wilderness for the next half century, but I fear if Englishmen do not go there, Yankees will."

"Joe, if you would know the meanness of human nature, you have to be a Prime Minister running a general election."

"Dear George, I propose, if you have no objection, to knock you into a cocked hat at the opening of Parliament next week. Yours Always, John."

"My greatest discovery was Thompson."

"Pacific in trouble, you should be here."

"Politics is a game requiring great coolness and utter abnegation of prejudice and personal feeling."

"Send me better men to deal with, and I will be a better man."

"The statement that this is a conquered country has been made so often is a propos de rein. Whether it was conquered or ceded, we have a constitution now under which all British subjects are in a position of absolute equality, having equal rights of every kind of language, of religion, of property and of person. There is no paramount race in this country, we are all British subjects and those of us who are not English are, none the less, British subjects on that count."

"We must always protect the rights of minorities and the rich are always fewer in number than the poor."

"Whatever you do, adhere to the Union. We are a great country and shall become one of the greatest in the universe if we preserve it. We shall sink into insignificance and adversity if we suffer it to be broken."

"With my utmost effort, with my last breath, I will oppose the veiled treason which attempts by sordid means and mercenary proffers to lure our people from their allegiance."

## Interview with Sir John A. Macdonald -- by Don Curtis

Open on set interviewer in a lounge chair facing Sir John A. Macdonald in matching chair. A fireplace in background.

INT: Good evening, my fellow Canadians. Tonight I have the distinct honour of speaking with Sir John A. Macdonald, the First Prime Minister of Canada and the father of Confederation, founder of the Northwest Mounted Police, builder of the Canadian Pacific Railway and chief architect of the BNA Act which created the Dominion of Canada. He served as Prime Minister for 19 years and served his country for half a century. A man who has been called the most influential and important politician in Canadian history. And the man who made Canada. Welcome Sir John.

JAM: Thank you for a very generous introduction. Indeed, it is my pleasure to be here.

INT: Perhaps, Sir John, we could start at the beginning; tell us when you came to Canada and why your family chose Kingston.

JAM: Certainly. I was born January 11, 1815 in Brunswick Place across the River Clyde from Glasgow, Scotland. My father registered my birth on January 15, which is the day I celebrate. My family emigrated to Kingston when I was five and I grew up there, as well as in Hay Bay and Adolphustown, Ontario. As to why Kingston, I was born the year of the battle of Waterloo, and following the war, Britain was plunged into a great depression forcing many Scots, Irish and British to emigrate for land, for work, and a for a better future for their families. Canada seemed to my father a place of great opportunity, as there were no class distinctions and I can still hear him say, *"John, a man can go as far as his talent and ambition will take him."* As to Kingston, there was a thriving Macdonald clan already here, and my mother Helen's step-sister was married to Colonel Donald MacPherson, a noted, military leader who had retired to Kingston after the war, so I guess you could say we had connections.

INT: Did you always want to be a politician?

JAM: (laughing) My mother was pushing in that direction. I articled for law starting at 15, went down to York and did an exam before a panel. The test was in Latin and English, as I recall; I passed, paid 15 pounds, and started as a law clerk with George McKenzie. Became a lawyer at 20 and started my own office that same year. One year too young to be admitted to the Bar. I ran for Kingston City Council in 1843, was elected to parliament in 1844, and was then elected to the legislative assembly of Canada West and Canada East. In 1867, I became Prime Minister following the passing of the BNA Act. But that all took twenty years.

But, I digress, back to your question...I guess, in truth, I was always a politician at heart. And fortunately, the voters of Kingston kept electing me. Except once, but that's another story.

INT: Just to go back to your own law office. I find it fascinating that you took on two law students, Alexander Campbell, who became a Member of Parliament, and Oliver Mowat, who became Premier of Ontario -- remarkable choices on your part for a young man.

JAM: Perhaps, but Campbell became a life-long friend, and Mowat a life-long enemy.

INT: I think it would be fair to state that without your vigorous fight throughout the 1860's, there would be no Canada.

JAM: Quite possibly. There were very serious American designs on Canadian lands; in fact, did you know that the U.S. government offered Britain $10 million for the Northwest Territories. I COULD NOT ALLOW THAT TO HAPPEN, and the future British Columbia was under extreme pressure to join the United States immediately after Confederation. My government began negotiation to purchase Rupert's Land and the Northwest Territories from the Hudson Bay Company...Got a good deal, too: 300,000 pounds! But all this turmoil and land threats are why the national Railway was so important. Well worth it, in hindsight.

INT: Harking back to the ongoing American threat, what role did Kingston play in your thinking?

JAM: Excellent and perceptive question. Kingston, as you know, was and is a garrison town, and we are constantly reminded of the American threat with soldiers ever present. Fort Henry was there and, of course, I shouldered a musket in 1837 to put down Mackenzie's rebels as part of the Loyal Scottish militia. And again in 1838 to defend Upper Canada from U.S. incursions by Hunter's Lodges. So, yes, I was more than aware of the constant threat and the need to have a strong unified country. All of this was a mere 25 years since President Madison and the War Hawks in congress declared war against British North America, and the threats were very real right up to Confederation.

INT: A seemingly dumb question, but why not just join the United States. You had two countries of similar people, most were from the British Isles, spoke a common language, many families had relatives on both sides of the border, and the U.S. was richer and stronger. Furthermore, the British government had indicated that they would not stand in Canada's way if we wanted to join the US.

JAM: **THERE WAS SOMETHING STANDING IN THE WAY!**

INT: And that would be?

JAM: **ME!**

INT: Ok, I think we'll go on to the next question. From an early age, you were a staunch advocate of a unified country. Would you say that was your primary political goal?

JAM: Absolutely true. I dedicated my political life to two main philosophies: i) to ensure the survival and growth of British North America through means of a colonial union; and ii) to build and maintain a viable east-west economy.

INT: Sir, if I may comment, by binding together a vast and sparsely populated country, you preserved the northern half of North America for your future fellow Canadians. A truly remarkable feat and we all thank you.

JAM: Thank you, I believe that we succeeded.

INT: Sir, you often refer to yourself as a Scotsman or a British subject. Do you consider yourself a Canadian?

JAM: I am Canadian at heart and soul. I have been in this country since I was five years old, my affections, my family are here, all my hopes and remembrances are Canadian; not only are my principles and prejudices Canadian, but my interests are Canadian.

INT: Speaking of Canadian, one of the most enduring symbols of Canada is what we now call the Royal Canadian Mounted Police, which I understand was your idea.

JAM: Correct, it was. And I decided that they should wear crimson coats in honour of the British army tradition. The original name was the North West Mounted Rifles, but I remember crossing out Rifles and substituting Police. And it was a good job that the force was around when the rebellions broke out, not to mention the Gold Rush. The train came in pretty handy, too. In fact, we were able to move troops to Manitoba in a record nine days, versus the 69 days it took for the Red River incident. The mounted police were crucial to bringing law and order to the west and in stopping the whiskey trade from the U.S. I am proud of the force and what they have done.

INT: Let's talk about the coalition, if I may call it that, with George Brown. Here we have two diametrically-opposed politicians coming together with a common purpose, to set aside a political deadlock and to build a nation. Quite amazing and very rare. Can you comment?

JAM: Yes, heady times called for clear heads. In 1864, the country was unstable. We had four governments in as many years; the British Government wanted to withdraw their troops and leave us to our own devices. And, of course, the U.S. was ever-present. The only solution was for a strong independent Canada under Britain's wing, so to speak, but as a country **we had to look unified and we had to look strong**. To achieve this, we had to have a colonial union and fortunately George Brown, who led the Reform Party, agreed. And we agreed to try and make it happen. I'll never forget myself, Brown, Cartier, Galt and McGee sailing together to Charlottetown on the government steamer to try and convince the Maritime colonies to join with Canada East and Canada West -- or Ontario and Quebec, as you may prefer -- to form a colonial union. And it was at that conference that the transcontinental railway was first discussed to eventually bring the west into the union.

We met four weeks later in Quebec and hammered out the details of the BNA Act. **I doubt that any other country in the world has done so, so quickly and so amicably. And it set the foundation of trust between the two founding cultures.**

INT: Was the population nervous of leaving the British fold?

JAM: Perhaps some were, but I tried to make it clear that we were not severing ties, and that the colonies were in transition. And gradually, year by year, it would be less a case of dependence on our part and of overruling protection on the part of the Mother country, and more of a case of a healthy and cordial alliance. Instead of looking on us as a merely dependent colony, England would have a friendly nation to stand with her in North America in peace and war. And as you know, that is exactly what transpired. Canadians have always remained loyal to the crown. In fact, loyalty may be the defining virtue of being Canadian. And it definitely distinguishes us from our neighbours to the south. Don't forget that a large part of our nation was settled by people we refer to as Loyalists, and whose spirit and traditions defined who we were and what we believed in -- God, Country and Crown.

INT: I note that in the matter of Confederation and again with building the railway, you did not hold an election on either issue, nor did you hold a referendum. Was this a lack of faith in the decision-making of the general populace?

JAM: (very angry) **MOST CERTAINLY NOT!!!** I always believed in the Canadian people's ability to make sound judgements. With regard to the Confederation debates, there was an urgency and to stump the country would have cost valuable time and inflamed emotions and made us look weak to the U.S. With regard to the railway, at the time we had a series of inconsequential elections, and it would have made no sense to have another. And I must add, that I have always believed that the people elect their parliamentary representatives to make decisions. What kind of representatives would we be if every time a decision was to be made, we ran to our constituents? No, it was our duty and our job to decide. And that is precisely what we did.

INT: Sir John, I don't want to bring up bad times, but you had a lot of personal tragedy in your life. Could you comment?

JAM: Yes, my first wife, Isabella, was bedridden for twelve of our fourteen years together, and we had a child die in infancy. Isabella passed away far too young. My second wife, Agnes, was a wonderful wife; but, unfortunately, our only child, Mary, was born with severe physical and mental difficulties. Of course, we are not the only family to face adversity.

INT: Sir, again, I don't want to dwell on the negative, but did those tragic events contribute to your drinking?

JAM: They probably did. No one is perfect and certainly not me. And I tended to drink when under great stress...not proud of it, but I did manage to still get the tasks at hand done. Proud of that!

INT: Any regrets in your illustrious career?

JAM: (sighs) Too many to even count. Politics is a game requiring great coolness and utter abnegation of prejudice and personal feeling. Can't claim a perfect record on either point. And, of course, my Scottish temper was never far from the surface.

INT: Speaking of Scots, there seems to be a lot of Scottish politicians in the Canadian government.

JAM: That is true. Did you realize that several of the fathers of Confederation were Scottish? Myself, George Brown, Alexander Galt, the first two Prime Minsters (myself and Alexander Mackenzie), and the first two premiers of Ontario, Oliver Mowat and John Sandfield Macdonald.

INT: Let's talk a bit more about the railway and the role it played in making Canada a country. If I may quote from a famous Canadian author by the name of Pierre Burton, *"In 1871, a tiny nation of just four years old, its population well below four million, determined to build the world's longest railway across empty country, most of it unexplored. The decision bold to the point of extreme, was to change the lives of every man, woman and child in Canada and alter the shape of the nation."* Comment?

JAM: I feel very strongly that until we completed the great work, our Dominion would be little more than a geographical expression, and you must remember that the negotiations were taking place during the American Civil War. The U.S. had a standing army of 600,000 trained and armed soldiers just south of the border, and a government calling for Manifest Destiny to take over all of North America. So as much as the building of a railway across thousands of empty miles seems foolhardy, there really was no choice if we were not to be swallowed up.

Railways changed everything. If memory serves, there were only 800 miles of track in Eastern Canada in 1854, and ten years later there were 3,000 miles and we could see the effect immediately. New towns and villages sprang up, cheaper goods were now available, not to mention fresher food. And, of course, the railway made the land more valuable. It was economically and politically wise to build a railway to bring the oceans together, and to increase interprovincial trade. **And I do believe that the boldness of the idea of a national railway somehow galvanized the** populace into a common dream and common purpose.

INT: The railway almost cost you your reputation. I refer to the Pacific Scandal. Comment?

JAM: In 1873, we were preparing for an election and I was focussed on making sure that we got British Columbia into Confederation. Pure and simple, I made a mistake of accepting election funds from Sir Hugh Allan, whom I was also negotiating with to head the railway. It looked wrong and my government was thrown out and reduced to 45 seats in the House. But the good people of Kingston stuck by me and I was personally re-elected. I was swept back to power in 1878, but this time I lost my seat...ah, the ebb and flow of politics.

INT: The National Policy returned you to power, correct?

JAM: We proposed a National Policy to build up Canadian manufacturing with tariffs, in effect making Canada master of its own economic affairs. And we recommitted ourselves to building the railway to the west coast in ten years. Thanks to William Van Horne, we did it in five.

INT: Is it true that in 1866, you and Lady Macdonald rode on the cowcatcher through Kicking Horse pass?

JAM: My wife suggested the idea, which I pronounced rather ridiculous and most dangerous, but she insisted and then convinced me against my better judgement to join her for a short spell. The things husbands do for their wives.

INT: While on this lighter note, let me read you a list of adjectives your contemporaries have said of you: audacious, clever, jolly, bad-tempered, courageous, drunk, debonair, jaded, vigorous, inflexible, sly, spindly, loyal, melancholic, perceptive, crotchety, conciliatory, wretched, resourceful, vain, congenial, autocratic, sensitive, deceitful, scoundrel and shrewd.

JAM: Guilty on all counts, and absolutely delighted that they care enough to even share an opinion pro or con.

INT: You faced another election in 1891.

JAM: Yes, and I was re-elected in Kingston. My son, Hugh, won a seat in the House in Winnipeg...A proud moment for a father.

INT: Sir, you were a strong proponent of the importance of protecting the French language and culture in Canada.

JAM: Yes, I was. But I was an even stronger proponent of our country. I have always said, **let us be English or let us be French, but above all let us be Canadian.** And I have not changed my view. **But I had no accord with the desire expressed in some quarters, that by any mode whatever, there should be an attempt to oppress one language or to render it inferior to the other. I believed that would be impossible if it were tried, and that would be foolish and wicked if it were possible.** And, of course, my great partner, Etienne Cartier, taught me the advantage of two cultures working together for the good of the country.

INT: I think that is a great quote to end the interview with. Thank You, Mr. Prime Minister. It has been an extreme honour and a pleasure.

JAM: It was my pleasure, I assure you.

(Fade to black and up. Interviewer is now sitting alone. The Sir John chair is now empty.)

INT: Sir John A. Macdonald died June 6th, 1891, at his residence in Ottawa. His body lay in state in the Senate Chamber, as Canadians from every walk of life filed by all day and far into the night of June 9th.

His funeral was attended by thousands, and many more thousands lined the railway tracks as his body was transported from Ottawa to Kingston. A requiem was held in Westminster Abbey in London, as were church services all across Canada. Sir John had promised his mother that he would be buried in the Cataraqui Cemetery in Kingston alongside his father, first wife, their infant son, and his two sisters.

As a special tribute, Queen Victoria raised Lady Agnes Macdonald in peerage to Baroness Macdonald of Earnscliffe.

I will close with a statement by Sir Wilfred Laurier, leader of the Opposition, who rose in the House with these words: **"The place of Sir John A. Macdonald in this country was so large and so absorbing that it is almost impossible to conceive that the politics of this country, the fate of this country, will continue without him. His loss overwhelms us. For my part, in all truth, his loss overwhelms me and it overwhelms this Parliament, as if indeed one of the institutions of the land has given way. Sir John A. Macdonald now belongs to the ages, and it can be said with certainty that the career which has just** closed is one of the most remarkable careers of tis century. As to his statesmanship, it is written in the history of Canada. It may be said without exception that the life of Sir John A. Macdonald, from the time he entered Parliament is the history of Canada."

Good night.

## Key points from Chapter 11

The amazing group of characters that strode our streets left an enduring legacy for all of us: Count Frontenac -- soldier, statesman and founder of Kingston; the amazing Molly Brant; the UEL, who chose our region and built a nation; John Stuart, founder of the Anglican religion in Canada.

And, of course, Sir John A. Macdonald. The first Prime Minister, the Father of Confederation, builder of the National Railway, founder of the Mounted Police, Chief Architect of the BNA Act of 1867.

**Opportunities:**

Kingston, as the Historic Heart of Canada, needs a museum to showcase these incredible people.

*"Learn to listen, opportunity may be knocking at your door, but very softly."*

# Chapter 12
# www.HistoryMoments.ca

## THE FASTEST GROWING HISTORY WEBSITE IN THE WORLD -- 1,000,000 VIEWINGS IN 90 DAYS!

History sells - worldwide. HistoryMoments.ca is a website dedicated to 60-second filmed vignettes about the history of Kingston and the region. In the spring of 2012, we launched a website through YouTube, featuring a dozen vignettes. Ninety days later we got an email from Google/YouTube stating that the site had over 1,000,000 viewings, and they declared it the fastest-growing history website in the world. People from virtually every other country in the world tuned in and watched history about Kingston. History sells. And our history excels.

The vignettes are:

1. Sir John A. Macdonald and the railway. Macdonald, the first Prime Minister of Canada had promised British Columbia on the west coast a railway in ten years if they joined the Canadian union. The job was completed in 5 years.
2. Sir John and the Mounted Police. Macdonald created the Northwest Mounted Police (later the Royal Canadian Mounted Police) to bring order to the Canadian west.
3. The Young John A. -- At 15, John Macdonald reports for his first day to study the law.
4. The Picton Trial -- 19-year-old John defended himself in an assault case and won. Had he lost the case, he would not have been eligible to be admitted to the Bar, and would not have become a lawyer, probably would never have made it to Parliament, never been Prime Minister...and who knows where Canada would be.
5. Lord Sydenham -- The first Governor General of Canada dies in office and is buried under the knave of St. George's Cathedral in Kingston, only weeks after vowing never to set foot in the church again.
6. Captain Michael Grass -- The British officer responsible for bringing the United Empire Loyalists to the Kingston area in 1794. Each family was given a plot of land as a gift from the Crown for their loyalty.
7. Nils Von Schoultz -- Captured at The Battle of the Windmill in Prescott, Ontario. Nils was tried at Fort Henry for an attack on Canada and was sentenced to hang. His ghost is said to walk the parapets at night.

8. Bishop Macdonnell -- A Catholic priest, he was charged with the responsibility of the Catholic faith from the Quebec border to the Manitoba border. He started the first Roman Catholic School in English, Regiopolos, in Kingston.
9. Charles Dickens in the Thousand Islands -- Dickens, famed British novelist, visited the region in the early 1840's. He didn't like Kingston (as it had had a major fire the year previous). But he waxed eloquently about the beauty of the Islands.
10. Billy Bishop at RMC -- World War I flying ace Billy Bishop attended the Royal Military College in Kingston. Billy left the college to fight in WWI. He joined the RAF and shot down 72 enemy planes, 5 in one day.

NOTE: Many other RMC alumni have served Canada in war and peace. Charles Merritt was a lawyer and military officer who won the Victoria Cross at Dieppe during the Second World War. Leonard Birchall, the "Saviour of Ceylon", discovered the approach of the Japanese fleet during the Second World War and showed courage and leadership as a prisoner of War in Japan. Other RMC alumni have had distinguished careers in the public and private sectors. Marc Garneau was the first Canadian in space, and is now a Member of Parliament. Chris Hadfield became a test pilot and an astronaut, and was the first Canadian to walk in space, and the first Canadian commander of the International Space Station. Jack Granatstein became a historian and headed the Canadian War Museum.

11. The Old 18 -- To this day, cadets at RMC must be able to recite the names and numbers of the original graduating class of the college. They were known as the Old 18.
12. WinstonChurchill in Kingston -- Winston Churchill visited Kingston in 1901 when the 26-year-old war hero was on a book tour.
13. Winston Churchill in Kingston -- In 1940, the British Prime Minister paid a top secret visit to Kingston to meet with Cordell Hull, Secretary of State in the Roosevelt Government to discuss the Lend Lease Agreement.

# Key points from Chapter 12

History and heritage sell and are a major worldwide draw for tourists.

www.HistoryMoments.ca attracted over 1,000,000 viewings worldwide in just 90 days.

Kingston stories sell, and we have hundreds to tell.

The media and production value of the site on the open market is estimated to be worth $18 million, at not one penny cost to the city.

Opportunity:
Keep telling our stories via TV vignettes. They work.

# Chapter 13
# The Loyalist Parkway / Birth of a Nation

THE UNITED EMPIRE LOYALISTS WHO SOUGHT REFUGE FROM THE AMERICAN REVOLUTION AND REMAINED LOYAL TO THE CROWN CAME TO CANADA STARTING IN 1784. IN EFFECT, THE AMERICAN REVOLUTION CREATED NOT ONE BUT TWO NATIONS. THE LOYALISTS BROUGHT WITH THEM BRITISH PARLIAMENTARY GOVERNMENT, BRITISH LAW AND BRITISH RELIGION (ANGLICANISM). THE UEL WERE OF GREAT SIGNIFICANCE TO CANADA AND, AS SUCH, SHOULD BE REMEMBERED AND CELEBRATED.

**Historic Plaques Trenton East**

1. The Bay of Quinte -- Carrying Place. In 1787, Sir John Johnson met with Mississauga chiefs to learn about alternate routes from Lake Ontario to Lake Huron.

2. The Kente Mission -- Established 1668, built by French Sculpicion priests to bring Christianity to the Iroquois.

3. Daniel Reynold's House -- Plaque is on the south side of Parkway in Wellington next to the church. Built in the 1790's, it is believed to be the oldest residence in the county. Reynolds was the first white settler in the region.

4. West Lake Boarding School -- Plaque on the north side of the Parkway between Picton and Bloomfield near Mallory Road. Site of a girls' boarding school established in 1841.

5. Hallowell -- Sir John A. Macdonald, the first Prime Minster of Canada, practiced law here in 1833. Plaque at the Post Office.

6. Founding of Hallowell -- The town merged with Picton in 1837. Hallowell was a Loyalist from Massachusetts. Plaque at Hill Street and Bay Street in Picton, east of the fairgrounds.

7. The Prince Edward County Fairgrounds 1836. North Main street Picton.

8. Paxton's Crystal Palace -- North of the Parkway on the west side of Hwy. 49 in the fairgrounds. Modelled on the London Crystal Palace of 1851. Built by Frank T. Wright in 1887. The only structure of its kind left in North America.

9. The White Chapel Church -- This is the first Methodist church in PEC and one of the earliest in Upper Canada. 3 km north of the Parkway on Hwy 49.

10. The County Registry Office, built in 1871; and Shire Hall, built in 1874 (Main St. north of the Parkway).

11. County Court House -- Union St., Picton. Built in 1832 on land donated by Rev. William Macaulay.

12. Macaulay Heritage Park -- Union and Church Streets, Picton.

13. Rev. William Macaulay -- 1794-1874, son of a Loyalist, ordained in 1818.

14. The Conference Church -- St. Mary's Street, Picton. Site of the first Methodist Church "Canada's Conference" 1824 resulting in the separation of the American and Canadian churches. A meeting here in 1831 settled the location of a Seminary of Learning at Cobourg. Later became Victoria University.

15. The Mills of Glenora, Lake On the Mountain Parkette. Plaque commemorates the founding of Glenora by Major Peter Asselstine. Sir John A. Macdonald's father lived here and ran a mill.

16. The Royal Union flag -- 1707-1801. The flag flies at the east end of the Glenora ferry dock. Was designed in 1606 by England and Scotland as their Royal standard commemorating the union of the thrones and parliaments of both countries. It consists of a blue background and a white diagonal cross of St. Andrew's, the patron saint of Scotland, with the superimposed red cross of St. George, the Patron Saint of England. **The Royal Standard became the flag of the United Empire Loyalists.**

17. Loyalist settlement at the Bay of Quinte -- east dock of the Glenora ferry. One of the first Loyalist settlements in Ontario (1783) populated by discharged soldiers and Loyalist refugees who were offered free land by the British government. Five townships were established between the Cataraqui River and the east end of the Isles of Quinte: Kingstown, Ernestown, Fredericksburg, Adolphustown and Marysburg. These other Loyalist settlements prompted the British Government to establish the

Province of Upper Canada.

**18.** The Loyalist Landing Place -- Adolphustown Park. Loyalists from New York landed here in June 1784 under the leadership of Major Peter Asselstine.

**19.** The Loyalist Memorial Church at Adolphustown. St. Paul's Church was built in 1822.

**20.** Quakers of Adolphustown -- plaque north of Adolphustown on the south shore of Hay Bay. The Quakers came here in 1785 and built their first Meeting House in 1795, holding the first Preparative Meeting of the Society of Friends of either Upper or Lower Canada in 1798. Be sure and see the names carved on the wall at the park.

**21.** Hay Bay Church -- North of Adolphustown and Dorland on the south shore of Hay Bay. The first Methodist Church in Upper Canada. Built in 1793.

**22.** Hazelton Spencer (1757-1813) - Plaque on the parkway west of Conway #9350. Spencer was a Loyalist from East Greenwich, Rhode Island. He was the first representative from the region elected to the Provincial Parliament, and an officer in the Royal Canadian Volunteer Regiment. He also served in the garrison at Kingston (1797-1799), and was commandant of Fort George (1800-1802). Appointed Lt. of the County of Lennox.

**23.** Rev. Robert McDowall (1786-1841). Plaque in Cemetery on north side of Parkway, Sandhurst. Came to Canada in 1798 and ministered to the Presbyterians in the Quinte area. He organized congregations in Ernestown, Adolphustown and Fredricksburg, and in so doing laid the foundation of Presbyterianism in Ontario. He died at Sandhurst and is buried there.

**24.** Lieutenant Colonel James Rogers -- Plaque at the church on the south side of the Parkway near Sandhurst. Born in Ireland, Rogers emigrated to Massachusetts with his family in 1730. A member of the Queen's Rangers during the Seven Year in the American Revolution, where he commanded the 2$^{nd}$ Battalion of the King's Rangers. In 1784, he led a contingent of 300 disbanded Rangers to the Sandhurst region.

**25.** Escape of the "Royal George" -- Plaque on the Parkway at County Rd. #8. Plaque reads, "There is the gap between Amherst Island and the eastern tip of the county. On November 9th, 1812, the Corvette Royal George (22 guns), commanded by Captain Hugh Earl, was intercepted off

False Duck Island by an American fleet of seven ships commanded by Commodore Isaac Chauncey. Pursued by the enemy, the Royal George escaped through the gap into the Bay of Quinte's northern channel. The chase resumed in light winds the following day and ended when she arrived safely in Kingston Harbour. Chauncey was intent on capturing such an important and large warship and attacked her in the harbour, but the shore batterys drove him off."

**26.** Finkle's Tavern -- Plaque on the Parkway at the west end of Bath. The Tavern was built in 1786 by Henry Finkle, a former Loyalist soldier as a stop between York and Kingston. Henry also built the first brewery in Upper Canada.

**27.** The Frontenac was the first steam-powered boat on the Great Lakes. Two years later, the Frontenac burned and sank in the Niagara River.

**28.** The Hawley House at Bath -- #531 Main Street. The house is the oldest house in the Bay of Quinte district. Built in 1785 by Captain Jeptha Hawley (1740-1813), a Loyalist from Arlington, Vermont. He joined the Royal D Standard in 1776, serving under General Burgoyne, and later was in charge of Loyalist refugees at Machiche, Quebec.

**29.** Reverend John Langhorn (1744-1817). Plaque north of the parkway at St. John's Church. The church and plaque are located cross the road from the former site of the Bath Academy. The plaque reads, *"Born in Wales, Langhorn was appointed missionary of Ernestown and Fredricksburg Townships in 1787. He thus became the first resident Anglican clergyman in the Bay of Quinte and the second in Ontario. Although an eccentric character, he proved to be a tireless supporter of his faith during the 26 years he served in the area. He was largely responsible for the erection of St. Paul's Church in Sandhurst in 1791, St. Warburg's in Fredricksburg in 1792, and the second St. John's in Bath (1793-95). He returned to England in 1813."*

**30.** The Founding of Bath -- Bath was founded in 1784 by discharged soldiers of Jessop's Rangers who were granted free land by the British Government. Originally called Ernestown, it was renamed Bath and incorporated as a village in the 1870's. It is one of the oldest communities in Ontario.

**31**. The Bath Academy -- Two blocks north of the Parkway. The plaque reads, "*Bath Academy 1811. On this site stood the Bath Academy, Lennox and Addington's earliest public school, founded in 1811 by means of local subscriptions. During the War of 1812 it was used as a military barracks. Barnabus Bidwell, a radical political reformer and supporter of William Lyon Mackenzie, was its first* *teacher*. The school was merged into the common system under The Public School Act of 1850.

**32.** Lt. Colonel Edwin Albert Baker (Baptist Church) -- Blinded in WWI, Baker was instrumental in founding the National Institute for the Blind, where he served for 44 years. He was elected President of the World Council for the Welfare of the Blind in 1951.

**33.** Madelaine de Roybon D'Allonne (1646-1718). Between Amherstview and Bath on the Parkway. A noblewoman from France, she became the first female landowner in Ontario, after it was granted to her by Sieur de LaSalle. She arrived at Fort Frontenac in 1679. Taken prisoner by the Iroquois in 1686, she was released a year later.

**34.** Fairfield House, Amherstview -- #4574 Parkway. Built in 1793 by William Fairfield and his wife Abigail. One of the few 18th Century Loyalist residences remaining in Ontario. They arrived in 1784 and finished building the house in 1793. The home remained in the family for six generations.

**35.** The Loyalist Parkway Eastern Gates -- The plaque reads, *"Loyalist Parkway recalls those Loyalists of diverse backgrounds who, during the American Revolution, had in common a proud allegiance to His Majesty King George III. Coming to this province from the United States for the most part in 1784, they provided a foundation for our growth."* The plaque commemorates the opening of the gateway in honour of the Loyalists. Officially opened by Queen Elizabeth on September 27, 1964.

# Key points from Chapter 13

**The coming of the United Empire Loyalists in 1784 created a nation.**

**It can be said that the American Revolution created two nations, not just one.**

**The coming of the Loyalists secured British control over the northern half of the North American continent.**

**The Loyalist Parkway represents an amazing historical tour through the heart of Loyalist country. The Loyalists are an important story that deserves to be better known.**

# Section 3
# Water, Water Everywhere

# Chapter 14
# Kingston's Blue Belt

## THE FINEST WATER LIFESTYLE IN NORTH AMERICA

**A GOLDMINE OF OPPORTUNITY FOR TOURISM AND ECONOMIC DEVELOPMENT.**

**TAKING A BIRD'S EYE VIEW OF THE REGION, YOU WILL SEE WATER, WATER, AND MORE WATER. WHERE OTHER CITIES BRAG ABOUT THEIR GREEN BELTS, KINGSTON HAS A WONDERFUL AND UNIQUE BLUE BELT OF FRESH WATER: LAKE ONTARIO TO THE SOUTH, THE BAY OF QUINTE TO THE WEST, THE MAGNIFICENT ST. LAWRENCE RIVER (AND THE INCOMPARABLE 1,000 ISLANDS) TO THE EAST, THE UNESCO WORLD HERITAGE RIDEAU CANAL TO THE NORTH...AND TO THE IMMEDIATE NORTH, OVER 5,000 BODIES OF WATER!**

Sail, boat, dive, fish, row, paddle, swim, windsurf and kiteboard. Whether you come to Kingston to live, work or play, we invite you to play in, on, or under our waters. Blessed by nature with strong winds, Kingston is recognized as **The Fresh Water Sailing Capital of the World.** Boating is unsurpassed, with immediate access to Lake Ontario, the St. Lawrence River and the 1000 Islands, the Rideau Canal and thousands of fresh water lakes for fishing, canoeing and kayaking. In fact, if you fished or paddled a different one of our lakes each week, it would take you 96 years to try them all. Just off our shores you can explore the wrecks of hundreds of sunken ships, a virtual underwater museum of the maritime life of the Great Lakes for over 300 years. These same waters have provided the life blood of Kingston, and now await you to experience their magic. They are why we believe that Kingston, Ontario, Canada offers the finest water lifestyle in all of North America. Let's explore the myriad of water activities that await the adventuresome.

## SAILING

As mentioned, Kingston is **The Fresh Water Sailing Capital of the World.** The prevailing winds and thermal breezes at the mouth of Lake Ontario are perfect for sailing. They are the reason we were chosen to host the 1976 Olympic sailing races, and why each year sailors of all ages come to Kingston to compete in CORK (Canadian Olympic Regatta, www.cork.org). And of course, recreational sailors are also here to enjoy the winds and the beauty of the area as well.

From Kingston harbour, you can sail anywhere in the world.

**West.** If you head west, you will pass the big Islands of Wolfe and Amherst and arrive at Prince Edward County with its sheltered bays, perfect for anchoring. Watch the sun go down over the calm waters as you prepare an evening meal. Travel a day further to enter the Trent-Severn waterway and you could be on your way to Georgian Bay.

**East.** Go east to the 1000 Islands and find a myriad of places to moor. The islands provide shelter for your boat, as well as a chance for a swim or walk through one of the 20 National Park Islands. And swap stories with any number of other boats anchored for the night. As you traverse any of the three channels through the islands, you may share the waters with huge tankers from exotic locations making their way up or down the St. Lawrence. And of course, you can go all the way up river to the Atlantic Ocean.

**South.** Go south and find Main Duck Island. Explore old farming settlements, or imagine rum runners of yesteryear who used the island as their depot. Continue on to Sacket's Harbor or Oswego, N.Y., or head up the Erie Canal to the dazzling lights of New York City.

**North.** Boat up the UNESCO World heritage site, the Rideau Canal, to Ottawa, our nation's capital.

North, south, east or west...choose a bearing and the world awaits. And all from the waters of Kingston!

# MARINAS

**Confederation Basin.** The municipal marina is in front of City Hall. Dozens of restaurants, grocery stores and services are within walking distance. Few cities have a marina in the heart of downtown like Kingston does. Depth is 14 feet, and there are 300 transient slips. Watch for the magnetic anomaly that makes compass readings in the marina vary, and watch out for shallow water near the Martello Tower (Shoal Tower).

**Portsmouth Olympic Harbour.** To the west of the city was the venue for the 1976 Olympic Sailing races. The marina is a municipal park with a playground and banquet facility. Most of the slips are held by seasonal boaters, but there are always a few transient slips available for people who want to overnight. The facility hosts numerous sailing regattas. www.cityofkingston.ca.

**Kingston Marina.** Located just under the causeway at the east end of the city on the eastern shore of the inner harbour. Part of a working dockyard; features 10 transient slips.

**Rideau Marina.** On the east shore of the Cataraqui River, north of the mouth.

**Collins Bay Marina.** West of the city. A great fuel stop with some opportunities to stay over. When approaching the marina, pay attention to the long shoal which extends from the most easterly of the Brothers Islands to Amherst Island. There are 70 transient slips and 300 seasonal dockage. www.collinsbaymarina.com.

**Treasure Island Marina.** 5 miles east of Kingston on the St. Lawrence.

Marine services and moorings can also be accessed at the Kingston Yacht Club, Bath and Loyalist Cove. For full marine services in the area, including sails, sail repair, boat retailers, marinas, outfitters, etc., go to www.cityofkingston.ca.

## RECREATIONAL SAILING

Whether you depend on the wind for power or prefer the deck of a powerboat, Kingston, Ontario offers boating enthusiasts unsurpassed diversity, beauty and experiences. Lake Ontario, the St. Lawrence River and the 1000 Islands, the Bay of Quinte or the Rideau Canal - whatever your choice, Kingston is truly a boaters' paradise.

Got a week to spare? How about working your way across the end of the big lake to Sacket's Harbor. On the way back, stop for a night at Main Duck Island, about 18 nautical miles from Kingston. Take a stroll along the shore and stop at the deserted lighthouse keeper's house. And consider a stop in Prince Edward County, which is becoming one of the great wine growing spots in Ontario.

Only have a day? Then why not sail along the shoreline of Kingston with its majestic views of the city, Fort Henry, The Royal Military College and the Kingston Penitentiary. Head out to into the 1000 Islands and stop at any of the 20 National Park islands, or have a picnic lunch aboard your boat in Deadman's Bay under the guns of Fort Henry.

Sailing through the 1000 Islands offers views of incomparable beauty with different vistas at every tack and turn. Swim, fish, dive and visit the bustling and historic shoreline towns on both sides of the river. **You can even attend a church service on your boat**. The list of things to do is virtually endless for those who venture forth into the fresh, clear, blue waters of Kingston.

Kingston residents often witness the site of two tall ships gracing our waters: the Fair Jeanne and the St. Lawrence II.

The "Fair Jeanne", a 110-foot replica of an 18th Century brigantine, carries over 4,000 feet of sail and is operated by Bytown Brigantine for sail training and character building for up to 30 youths age 14-24. The ship was built in 1982 by the late Captain Charles Fuller as a private yacht. Captain Fuller was one of the most decorated heroes of WWII, earning the nickname, "Pirate of the Adriatic", and he holds the distinction of the longest time served in offensive war action. His wartime experiences taught him the value of installing confidence and resourcefulness in youth through adventure at sea. www.tallshipsadventure.org.

The "St. Lawrence II", Portsmouth Olympic Harbour, Kingston. The St. Lawrence II was built in 1952 by Francis MacLachlan and Mike Earnes, expressly for youth training. The hull was built by the Kingston Shipyards and finished by local craftsmen and Sea Cadets. The ship is 72 feet long, has a deck length of 60 feet and a beam of 15 feet. The sails measure 2,500 square feet. On board training sessions for boys and girls ages 12 to 18 run six to ten days. The ship can accommodate a crew of 25. Working on board the St.Lawrence instills discipline, self-esteem, self-reliance, responsibility, and the value of team work. www.brigantine.ca

Watching either of these tall ships and their young crews sail by the city is always an awe-inspiring sight.

## COMPETITIVE SAILING

Kingston's huge harbour, its warm, fresh waters and its almost guaranteed winds meld to make racing sailboats a unique, world-class experience. For years, local sailors recognized the perfect sailing conditions and as the rest of the world took note, Kingston became the **The Fresh Water Sailing Capital of the World**. This reputation was enhanced when the Canadian Olympic committee chose Kingston as the site of all of the 1976 Olympic sailing events. Since that time, Kingston has played host to over 100 major sailing competitions all centered at Portsmouth Olympic Harbour. The harbour can accommodate as many as six racing circles at a time and, of course, the thermal winds arrive daily. Unlike almost every other sailing venue, the water is fresh and clear with temperatures in the mid-20's Celsius (70's Fahrenheit), and sea conditions can be very exciting.

And with a major city core just minutes away, on-shore activities and boating facilities are readily available.

## CORK -- THE CANADIAN OLYMPIC REGATTA KINGSTON

As community festivals go, CORK (www.cork.org) is extremely important to the city and the entire sailing world. With a group of over 300 dedicated volunteers who arrive in the city from all over Canada and beyond. CORK has few equals anywhere as a world-class regatta. CORK began in 1969, and with careful guidance of Kingstonians and key Canadian sailors, it has become known as the world's largest and best run regatta, hosting well over 1,000 boats in the 1990's.

Today, CORK is a two-week sailing festival hosting events for children in Optimist dinghies to "big boat" sailors in offshore divisions. It is "regatta central" for hundreds of youth at the annual YOUTH FESTIVAL, and for competitive dinghy racers from as many as 15 classes.

What an opportunity for young sailors to race alongside world racing champions!

In most sailors' calendars, the second two weeks in August are blocked off for a year in advance because it's sailing time in Kingston, and there will be a gathering-of-the-clan at CORK.

# WINDSURFING AND KITEBOARDING

The same great winds that attract sailors from all over the world make Kingston ideal for windsurfing and kite boarding, too!

To have a really first-class "boarding" site, there must be easy access and free access to clear navigable waters, reliable wind for all levels, long warm summers -- by donning wetsuits, the season lasts from April through November -- and for good measure, a windsurfing school, shoreline ambiance for apres sail sessions, a friendly local community of boarders and kiters, and regular regattas. **Fortunately, Kingston has all of these and more!** Not to mention not having to wash the salt off everything as in ocean surfing.

The city's waterfront is largely public space and boarders gather at Richardson Beach -- home base of some of the best windsurfing in Canada. Less than a kilometre west, is the kite boarders' site of choice across the road from Queen's University, making it popular with students. Using the power of nature, kiteboarders can lift themselves 30 feet in the air or skim along the surface at breathtaking speeds. The Kite acts as both a lifting and pulling force, allowing the boarder to launch dramatic aerial manoeuvres.

When the wind is up, a local network gets on the phone to say, "the vegetation is moving" and, almost immediately, windsurfers appear in the park. Visitors can check with the local Yacht Club for conditions or just drop by the waterfront. Everyone is welcome.

# POWER BOATING

Boating through the Thousand Islands is one of boating's great adventures, with a different and magnificent view at every turn in the river you will be thrilled with and amazed at. Sightsee and visit quaint towns on both sides of the river, looking for castles, cottages and cannons. Picnic on any of the 20 National Park Islands. Swim, dive and fish -- the world's record Muskelunge was caught right at the mouth of the St. Lawrence by Lake Ontario. You can even attend church from your boat.

COMPETITIVE BOATING -- THE POKER RUN

When it comes to power boating -- and we mean POWER -- every August Kingston hosts The 1000 Islands Poker Run, one of the summer's most popular events. Boating enthusiasts flock to the waterfront to see these huge, colourful and powerful boats.

The event begins on Friday with state of the art speedsters displayed in front of City Hall. On Saturday, the boats leave Kingston for Rockport, Brockville, and Prescott, before heading back to Kingston, picking up a card in each location. The winner is the one returning with the best poker hand.

# RECREATIONAL BOATING

Did you know that there are actually 1,864 islands in The 1,000 Islands? Here, you will find Canada'a smallest National Park -- the St. Lawrence National Park -- established in 1904. The first National Park East of the Rockies with 20 islands, many with moorings and camp sites, but all available to explore. Enjoy Adelaide Island with 2 moorings, Camelot with 6 moorings, Endymion with 7 moorings, as well as Leek Island and Beaurivage Island. Try the beach at Central Grenadier or Potter's Beach opposite Leek Island. There is a non-denominational church service every Sunday at 4:30 all summer long at Half Moon Bay at the south end of Bostwick Island 2.5 kilometres west of Gananoque narrows. For hiking and biking enthusiasts, there is a 37-kilometre path along the Canadian side.

Departing Kingston, there are three main channel routes through the islands. Charts are available at a number of Kingston outlets.

The middle channel will take you through the heart of the Islands on the Canadian side, with a relatively clear run to Rockport, where you will find full marine services. Or you can choose to travel along the north shore of Wolfe Island through the Simcoe Island channel to Lake Ontario. The crossover to the main shipping channel is on the U.S. side of Wolfe Island. Finally, there is a Canadian Middle Channel that will take you north of Howe Island in the Bateau Channel along the shoreline. At Gananoque, find full marine services. The Canadian Middle channel meets up with the inside channel at Gananoque narrows.

En route to Brockville, travel along the small craft route between Tar Island and Grenadier Island and thread the Brockville narrows. Near Prescott, you will see the first lock of the St. Lawrence Seaway at Iroquois, east of Morrisburg. Here, you will pass several waterfront communities including Cornwall, Summertown, Lancaster and Bainsville. All offer slips and shopping.

## THE RIDEAU CANAL

A UNESCO World Heritage site...an historic journey, beyond beauty. For a totally different, but equally rewarding, boating experience. **The Canal is Canada's and North America's oldest regularly operating canal.** It links the St. Lawrence River and Ottawa River, and was designed by engineers from Britain, built 1827-1834 under the supervision of Colonel By, the founder of Ottawa. The canal handles over 90,000 boats a year. The Rideau Canal celebrated its 175th anniversary in 2007.

The 202-kilometre (125-mile) journey will take 3 to 5 days, traversing numerous lakes and passing through 47 locks and 22 stations. Each lock is 1,344 feet long and 33 feet wide. Permits and charts are available at the lock stations. Vessel draughts should not exceed 1.2 metres or 4 feet. The canal is open late May to mid-October. Call 613-283-5170, or visit the website at www.rideau-info.com/canal.

# THE TRIP THROUGH THE CANAL

From Kingston, pass under the La Salle Causeway (larger boats will have to wait for the bridge to be raised). Head north on the Cataraqui River to the first lock at Kingston Mills, then on to Lower and Upper Brewers. Leaving Upper Brewers, you enter Cranberry lake (excellent pike and bass fishing).

The bridge at Brass Point has a clearance of 1.5 metres (4 feet). The channel on the northeast leads to Seeley's Bay. Be sure to consult your charts regarding the coloured markers here. There is a government dock and nearby grocery, liquor and beer store. Seeley's Bay was created during the building of the canal when Cranberry Marsh was flooded. The sheltered harbour and launch area lead to a long stretch of the Rideau without locks, and is ideal for fishing and sightseeing. There is also a sheltered anchorage to the southeast with a mud bottom clearance of 4 -5 metres (12-19 feet).

Then on to Jones Falls and shopping, trails and swimming ponds. The stone dam at Jones Falls was the highest in the world when built in 1832-33. It is 350 feet by 60 feet, and requires four locks to raise and lower the boats.

Proceed along the waterway to Davis Locks and Chaffey's Locks (full marine services). Proceed through Indian Clear and Newboro Lakes to the Newboro Locks. Note that the canal at Newboro narrows. Colonel By Island in Big Rideau Lake offers washrooms, BBQ, picnic tables and 48-hour camping for boaters.

Situated on an isthmus between Newboro Lake and the Upper Rideau, it marks the watershed divide between the waters flowing north to Ottawa and the waters flowing south to Kingston. On the west end of Upper Rideau, Newboro Lake and the canal are a gateway to some of the finest bass and trout fishing in all of Eastern Ontario. Westport harbour marina has dock space for transient boaters as well as great fishing. In Westport, note the boaters' beach a short distance down the lake. Also visit Foley's Mountain Park, with 600 acres of woods and fields. The 300-kilometre Rideau Trail from Kingston to Ottawa loops around Westport.

At the south end of Big Rideau Lake, Portland offers banking, shopping, a liquor store, laundromat and full marine services. As you are now in the Rideau Lakes, fishing is great, while camping and sightseeing are a must. For an interesting side trip, head to Beveridge Locks and take the Tay River to historic Perth, often referred to as "the prettiest town in Ontario". Perth was founded in 1816. Back in the main canal, head to Smiths Falls where you will find the Rideau Canal head office and the Rideau Canal museum.

Overnight docking at Victoria Basin, in-town campgrounds on 300 acres, shore fishing, swimming, walking tours, picnicking, cycling and hiking trails.

Proceed through Edmonds, Kilmamock and Clowes Locks to Merrickville, known as "the jewel of the Rideau", founded in 1783 and graced with 19th Century architecture, including many unusual boutiques and inns. Full service marina just below the locks. Check out the Migratory Bird Sanctuary on the western edge of town. From here you will pass through Nicholson's Locks and Burritts Lock, a good place to swim and hike along the walking path to town. At Baekett's Landing, you can check out Ludlow Boat Works, where Canada's oldest registered sailing vessel is being restored -- 100 years old in 2007.

Next you will pass through Long Islands, Black Rapids, Hogs Back and Hartwell's Locks, before reaching the end of your journey at the nation's Capital, Ottawa. You can tie up along the canal (24-hour docking), and explore downtown Ottawa, including many museums and art galleries.

# DIVING

Kingston is recognized as one of the best dive sites in North America. Our 340-year maritime history dating from 1673 has resulted in a virtual underwater museum. It is believed that there are about 1,000 sunken ships between Brockville and Picton, many right off the shores of Kingston.

During the War of 1812, Kingston became the site of the Royal Dockyards. To the northeast are the watery graves of several old steamships. At least 10 vessels lie in the two main graveyards southeast of Amherst Island and southwest of Simcoe Island. Many of the sunken ships in our waters are schooners, the workhorse of the marine trade of the late 1800's and early 1900's. The harbour features a number of wrecks including the Wolfe Islander II, now an artificial reef for divers. The sunken ships of Kingston represent some of the best and only surviving examples of several of these classes of boats that plied the Great Lakes. Excellent photos can be found at Vlada Dekina's website (www.wrecksandreefs.com/ontario.htm). To ensure the preservation, Preserve Our Wrecks (POW) (www.gtcs.org/pow.htm) was formed in 1981 to supervise a mooring program for 15 of the most popular dive sites. The moorings are for the safety of the divers. There are dozens of local companies dedicated to providing rental equipment, air refills and charter boat services.

# THE WRECKS

**"The Wolfe Islander II"** -- A coastal freighter built in Collingwood in 1946 and converted to a side-loading car ferry. It was sunk as an artificial reef in 1985. She is intact and diver-friendly, as all door and hatches have been pinned back. There are two permanent moorings.

**"The Comet"** -- A steam-powered sidewheeler built in Portsmouth Village in 1848. Legends of a curse surround the ship. In 1849, a burst steam pipe killed two crew; a boiler exploded in 1851 killing eight; and, in 1861, the ship collided with the Schooner Exchange southwest of Nine Mile Point and sank in 80 feet of water. Adding to the ships's curse, two men were thrown from a lifeboat and drowned. The Comet was the finest and the earliest example of marine engineering in Central Canada featuring the typical types of engines that powered pre-Confederation vessels. Its main deck and machinery and walking beam are intact, and two paddle wheels rise 25 feet from the bottom. There is a permanent mooring.

**"HMS Wolfe"** -- Launched in 1813 at the Kingston Dockyards and originally named the Sir George Prevost after the Governor General of Canada at the time. He ordered construction of Canadian warships in response to American ships being built at Sacket's Harbor, N.Y. The "Wolfe" was a 20-gun sloop of war with a crew of 220. It was badly damaged by the USS General Pike, but Commodore Yeo was able to escape and get to Kingston for repair. In the winter of 1813-14, the ship was renamed HMS Montreal and involved in the raid on Fort Oswego. After the war, it became a cargo ship. Its final resting place is near RMC and is known as Gauntier's Wreck.

**"George A. Marsh"** -- A three-masted schooner with a registered tonnage of 220 was built in Muskegon, Michigan in 1882 and met her fate in a 1917 gale while hauling 450 tons of coal from Oswego to Kingston. Of the 12 people on board, only two survived. It sits upright in 75 feet of water, and is characterized by the ship's wheel, bow sprit and many deadeyes. There are also two fallen masts, riggings, spars, a lifeboat, tools on the deck and a windlass on the bow. Permanent mooring provided.

**"The Munson"**- An excellent example of an early working dredge, it sank in 110 feet of water in 1890. The wreck features two decks, engine boiler, steam shovel, electric generator, workshop, porcelain and enamel artifacts.

**"Aloha"** and **"Effie Mae"** -- Two wrecks, 15 feet apart. The "Aloha" was built in 1888 at Mt. Clemens, Michigan, and was under American enrollment until 1913 when it assumed Canadian registration. Under tow, the vessel was hauling 925 tons of coal when she floundered abreast of Nine Mile Point, Simcoe Island. It rests upright in 55 feet of water on a sandy flat bottom, and is generally intact from stem to stern. The "Effie Mae" is a 40-foot wooden trawler built in the 1960's, and was Kingston's first dive charter boat. She was sunk as a dive site in 1994. Two permanent moorings.

"**City of Sheboygan**" -- A three-masted schooner built in 1871 in Sheboygan and registered in Canada in 1915. She sank that same year while on route to Buffalo with 500 tons of feldspar, when a gale swept in and doomed the ship. The Captain, his wife, and three hands perished. Sitting in 90 feet of water, the wreck features a large hull. Many pieces of rigging can be seen and other features include a raised forecastle deck with capstan, catheads and pintail, a steam winch and donkey boiler, an anchor, windlass and anchor chain.

"**KPH**" -- Named KPH because of its proximity to the Kingston Psychiatric Hospital, the wreck is an unidentified flat barge sitting upright in 65 feet of water, with hull intact from stem to stern.

## AMHERST ISLAND GRAVEYARD

"**The Cornwall**" -- This iron-hulled sidewheeler was launched in Montreal in 1854 as "The Kingston", and was considered the finest of Canadian steamships of her day. Chosen as the Prince of Wales floating Palace during his visit in 1860. The ship was gutted by fire in 1872 and rebuilt (as the Bavarian), only to burn again in 1885. In 1895, she was renamed Cornwall, converted to a tender ship in 1911 and scuttled in 1931. It lies in 75 feet of water with wheels and machinery intact, as well as most of its bow section.

"**The Glenora**" -- One of the unidentified wooden steamers in the graveyard, the ship was given the name by local divers. Its hull sits upright in 75 feet of water and has many swim-throughs and hidden secrets.

"**The Titanic**" -- So called because it is the largest of the Amherst Island wrecks. Divers are awe-struck by the sheer size of the steamer's skeleton and debris field.

## DUCK ISLANDS

"**Annie Falconer**" -- A three-masted schooner built in Picton in 1871, it was used primarily as a barley carrier. The ship sank in 1880, and all six hands on board perished.

**"The Olive Branch"** -- A schooner built in 1867 in Kingston, it sank during a storm in 1904.

**"The R.H. Rae"** -- A well-equipped and superbly finished barge built in St. Catharines in 1857. It capsized in a squall the following year.

# FISHING

The Kingston region has two main types of fishing. You can head out into the big waters of Lake Ontario to fish off Wolfe Island or Main Duck Island, or you can revel in the beauty and serenity of the back lakes, creeks and rivers of the region. And, of course, don't forget the mighty St. Lawrence River itself.

Lake Ontario fishing is often compared to ocean fishing or fishing in the extreme north, as the waters are deep and cold. Fishing is best in summer, but the months of April and May bring the early brown trout into the shallows to feed on spawning baitfish. Chinook salmon and lake trout find their way to shore to put on pounds after a long winter. June, July and August bring the larger Chinook and king salmon (15 pounds in spring to 40 pounds in fall). Other species include Coho salmon, large and small mouth bass, muskellunge, steelhead, walleye, rainbow trout and Atlantic salmon. The worlds's largest muskellunge was caught just east of the city, weighing in at 69 pounds. The fishing is world-class and yearly attracts anglers from the U.S., Quebec, Germany, Switzerland, Sweden, Norway and even Guatemala. The depth of the water and the deep fishing techniques result in salmon caught 85 feet down and requiring one hour to land. Fishermen and women from around the world make their way to the deep, fresh blue waters of Kingston to catch the "big ones". The experience will leave you breathless. If you fished a different one of our lakes once a week, it would take you 96 years to fish them all!

## BACK LAKE FISHING

A quick look at a map of the Kingston area will show a myriad of lakes just to our north. In fact, there are 5,000 bodies of water with 38 lakes within a one hour drive of City Hall. And they are brimming with fresh water fish. I asked a local fisherman to pick his ten favourite lakes, and here they are:

**Big Rideau Lake**
**Whitefish Lake:** bass, pike, crappie
**Loughborough Lake:** trout, pike, bass, perch, splake
**Dog Lake:** trout, bass, pike, perch, splake
**Collins Lake:** walleye, northern pike, bass, perch, muskie

**Devil Lake:** walleye, northern pike, bass, perch
**Buck Lake:** walleye, northern pike, bass, perch
**Sharbot Lake:** trout, walleye, northern pike, bass, perch
**Beaver Lake:** walleye, northern pike, bass
**Gould Lake:** trout, walleye, bass, perch

# ROWING

Row, row, row your boat, gently or not so gently down the Cataraqui River. On any given morning, as the mist breaks over the river, you will find teams of rowers of all ages, their long blades sliding through the water as they silently slip by at breath-taking speeds. Teamwork and dedication show on their faces, and they have the results to prove their hard work has been worth the effort.

The Kingston Rowing Club is a key member of Canada's rowing community. Its members are rowers of all ages, from pre-teens to seniors, who row for purely recreational reasons or to compete in world class competitions.

The first competitive rowing in Kingston was held in 1837 on the Cataraqui River. In the 1870's, a resurgence of rowing took place in Kingston, stemming from the popularity of five-time world champion Ned Hanlan (whose parents lived for a time in Kingston). On April 25, 1881, the Kingston Rowing Club was officially founded and held its first regatta on Dominion Day of that year.

Getting started as a rower is easy. It is a sport anyone can enjoy, and in which beginners progress rapidly. And it brings significant health benefits, because it exercises all major muscle groups through a full range of motion.

#1 Cataraqui Street opposite the River Mill Restaurant.
www.rowkingston.on.ca or www.rowingcanada.org.

## KINGSTON ROWING CLUBS

High School rowing: KCVI, Ernestown, Regiopolos and Frontenac participate at the novice, junior and senior levels. Each year, the high school rowers compete at the Canadian High School Championships.

College rowing: The Queen's University team boasts 60 Varsity rowers, 40 competitive rowers, and 2,000 recreational rowers. The team competes along with 11 other universities at the Canadian Nationals. The highlight of the season is the annual trip to Boston for the Head of Charles Regatta, the

Boston Marathon of rowing.

Community-based rowing: The club sponsors various programs including spring and fall training sessions, learn to row, youth summer rowing camps in July and August, and the Rowing League for recreational rowers with weekly races and a meet and greet afterward. The oldest rower is in his 70's.

# PADDLING

Canoes and Kayaks...Pierre Berton once said that you hadn't seen Canada until you have seen it from the seat of a canoe.

If paddling is your sport of choice, then start your journey here in Kingston where there is no end of beautiful places to dip your paddle.

The Cataraqui Canoe Club is conveniently located next to the Kingston Rowing Club on Cataraqui Street adjacent to the Woolen Mill. The club offers a chance to canoe or kayak evenings and Saturdays on the Cataraqui River, as well as weekend excursions to area waterways. Also offered are whitewater experiences in the spring and fall, as well as racing in association with the Sydenham Canoe Club. Additionally, the club coordinates a program for the Boys & Girls Club of Kingston.
www.cataraquixcanoeclub.on.ca.

## FRONTENAC PARK

Canada's most southerly wilderness park is only 30 minutes away, with superb canoeing and kayaking in any of its 22 lakes. As part of the Canadian Shield and the Frontenac Axis, the park is designated a UNESCO World Heritage site.

To the east is Charleston Lake Provincial Park, and to the northeast Bon Echo Provincial Park, both of which offer great paddling, fishing and hiking.

## PADDLING THE PARKS

Less than one hour north of Kingston is some of the finest canoeing in all of Canada. If you like paddling from lake to lake without need of a portage, the Depot Lakes await. Canoe for over 75 kilometers and only lift your canoe around a couple of dams. You can rent a canoe or kayak right at the mouth of the park from Frontenac Outfitters, and the equipment is top notch.

# KAYAKING

Of course, the same waters described above are just as wonderful for kayaking, especially in spring when white water can be found and experienced. In addition, the Thousand Islands are becoming a world-class kayaking destination with endless day and extended trips though quiet bays, meandering channels and thrilling open waters.

Kayaking is an ideal way to enjoy the natural charm of the region. Narrow passages, deep marshes or alongside sheer granite cliffs, kayaks enable you direct access to places rarely seen by motorized boats.

Last but not least, you can paddle the entire length of the Rideau Canal...it will take you about 5 days.

# A BIT MORE ABOUT HIKING...

### FRONTENAC PARK

You can go for a hike in 15,000 acres of wilderness, less than an hour from City Hall. The park is considered one of the finest hiking parks in Ontario. The 160 kilometres of trails are clearly marked and are laid out in convenient loops ranging from simple 1.5 kilometres to challenging 20+ kilometre hikes that wind through forests, lake shores, hills, waterfalls, gorges and historic sites. Knowledgable staff at the Trail Centre will explain all the trails and gauge your ability for each one. Wilderness courses are offered all year long. No powerboats, ATVs or bicycles are allowed.

Most trails are accessible from Salmon Lake Road in the park. Several trails are ideal for cross-cross country skiing or snowshoeing in winter. A trip to the park will reveal billion-year-old outcrops, 22 lakes, 48 interior campsites, 29 species of mammals, 170 species of birds, 9 species of snakes, and 7 species of turtles.

### TRAILS IN FRONTENAC PARK

**Arab Lake Gorge Loop** -- 1.5 km, approximate time 40 minutes. Boardwalk with close-up of flora and fauna on the gorge. Directly accessible from the Trail Centre.

**Arkon Lake Loop** -- 13 km, 1.6 km from the Trail Centre, 3.5-hour hike on the west of the park. Excellent views of Arkon and Birch Lakes and the adjacent hills.

**Big Salmon Lake Loop** -- 19 km from the Trail Centre, hiking time 5-7 hours. Around the shoreline of Big Salmon. Several lookouts.

**Hemlock Lake Loop** -- 11 km, 7.5 km from Trail Centre, hiking time 3-5 hours. Old logging road, geology of the Hardwood Bay area of Devil's Lake. Note the site of the old logging shanty near Hardwood Bay.

**Little Clear Lake Loop** -- 9 km, 6.5 km from Trail Centre, hiking time 3-6 hours. Several abandoned homesites from the 1800's.

**Little Salmon Lake Loop** -- 15 km, 2 km from Trail Centre. Excellent views of Moulton Lake.

**Slide Lake Loop** -- 21 km, 3.3 km from Trail Centre, hiking time 6-8 hours. Most rugged part of the park. Crosses Labelle Gorge and passes waterfalls that drop 16 metres from Slide Lake to Buck Lake. Experience excellent views of Mink and Camel Lakes, as well as the ridge and trough area of the park. The short version of the loop circles beautiful Slide Lake. Access from the east side at Perth Road Village and through the Rideau Trail.

**Tetsmine Lake Loop** -- 12 km, 8.6 km from Trail Centre, hiking time 4-6 hours. North zone of the park. Marble ridges, rock outcrops, mature deciduous forests, abandoned mica mines and the remains of the McNally homestead on Kingsford Lake.

**Doe Lake Loop** -- 3 km, accessible from Trail Centre, hiking time 1-2 hours. Skirts two beaver ponds. Climb to a spectacular lookout over Doe Lake and return along the shoreline of Otter Lake.

OTHER TRAILS TO EXPLORE

**The Birch Lake Trail** -- 3 km. Linking Tetsmine Lake Loop and the Arkon Lake Loop, following the shoreline of Birch Lake.

**The Bullhead Trail** -- Bisects the Arkon Lake Loop providing an opportunity for visitors to hike a loop starting and ending at the Arkon parking lot.

**The Corridor Trail** -- Starts at the Trail Centre and goes north to Big Salmon Lake and leads to other loops. Popular for cross-country skiing.

To get to Frontenac Park from Hwy 401, take exit 613 (Sydenham Rd.) and travel north to Sydenham. Follow signs to Park www.ontarioparks.com/

english/fron.html. For map, see www.ontarioparks.com/english/fron-maps.html.

## THE RIDEAU TRAIL

The Rideau Trail is 300 kilometres long and joins Ottawa and Kingston. It is designated by orange triangles, and passes through the southerly section of Frontenac Park.

## LITTLE CATARAQUI CREEK CONSERVATION AREA

Closer to home is Little "Cat", right in the City of Kingston...394 acres of marsh, fields and forest. Offers hiking, canoe rentals, picnicking and in winter features snowshoeing, cross-county skiing, and skating on the region's largest natural skating rink. North on Division Street.

## LEMOINE POINT PARK

Lemoine Point Park. At the west end of Kingston off Bayridge Drive. 337 acres with forests and hiking trails, playground.

*"Dawn breaks a thin horizontal blue-grey over the nearby treetops to the east. Overhead, stars continue to shimmer against a black sky as the ferry Wolfe Islander III prepares for another day of 19 round trips. Cars have been lining up steadily from the dock, up and along the village of Marysville's main street since 5:00 AM, each one waiting for their turn to board upon a signal from the crew. If you listen closely, you can hear the sudden whoosh of air which, in turn, starts each of the ferry's four engines, one at a time. The propellors, both fore and aft, disturb the water of the bay into a whirlpool of eddies and currents, all flowing at a forty degree angle from her starboard side. It is still dark in this early morning air, as deck flood lights blink on, lighting the five-car lane deck which will soon be crowded with about 50 cars and probably a tractor-trailer or two. After 30 reliable years, the Wolfe Islander III continues to link the largest island in the Thousand Islands to nearby Kingston. From a distance, her gleaming white silhouette with twin smoke stacks is as familiar as any waterfront monument in historic Kingston as she makes her way across the channel. Every trip, three nautical miles of eastern Lake Ontario pass under her keel as she ploughs through thick winter ice, spring thaw with fog and moving ice floes, gentle summer breezes and late fall gales in perfect safety."*

-- Brian Johnson, Captain, Wolfe Islander III

# Key points from Chapter 14

Kingston's unique Blue Belt of clear fresh water is the city's #1 asset for tourism and economic development.

The Blue Belt represents the finest water lifestyle in North America.

The waters of Kingston deliver many water sports.

These sports are a key element in attracting new residents and tourists to the city and the region.

*"No great man ever complains about the work of opportunity." - Emerson*

# Chapter 15
# Kingston's Other Waterfront

We tend to think of Kingston's waterfront as that stretch of land from the causeway along Lake Ontario to the Richardson Wharf. But there is another waterfront with an important history of its own, commonly known as the inner harbour.

We begin our story at the tourist office in the outer harbour. The building was the station for the Kingston & Pembroke Railway, the K&P or, as it was known in its day, The Kick and Push.

Downtown Kingston at the turn of the century would look vastly different from that of today. Five-ton steam engines belching steam rolled noisily right into downtown off-loading lumber, coal and wheat, which were transferred to Great Lake freighters and barges for points throughout the Great Lakes and up the St. Lawrence River. The K&P railway was incorporated in 1871 to gain access to the natural logging and mining resources north of the city. In 1882, James Richardson erected a huge grain elevator at the foot of Princess Street with a capacity of 60,000 bushels, rebuilding it in 1898 to hold 250,000 bushels. And the Montreal Transportation Company erected another elevator at the foot of Queen Street with a capacity of 800,000 bushels. Adding to the bustling economy, there were two shipbuilding yards, a marine railway, a rope works, blacksmiths, sail loft, two drydocks, 10 steamship agencies, a yacht fitter, three large forwarding companies, several chandlers and six marine insurance companies.

The K&P Railway was leased to the Canadian Pacific Railway in 1912 for 999 years. The entire line was abandoned in parts in 1962, 64, 66, 77 and 1986. Parts of the rail bed now form the K&P trail, and are part of the Inner Harbour Heritage Trail. Heading east, we come to the La Salle Causeway and the mouth of the Cataraqui River, and the beginning of the Inner Harbour tour.

**The Kingston Inner Harbour Heritage Trail -- a step back in time and a pathway to our Native, French, British, Industrial and natural heritage.**

**The La Salle Causeway**, known to local children as the "singing bridge" because of the high-pitched ringing sounds of the car tires on the metal bridge. As early as 1789, Richard Cartwright (one of the original Loyalists) operated a ferry service from Kingston to Point Frederick. Prior to the War of 1812, a road ran from Brockville to Middle Road, Pittsburg Township up to Kingston Mills and back down Montreal Street to Kingston. Construction of the Penny Bridge began in 1827, vastly shortening the route from York to Montreal. The bridge originally had a toll of 2 pence, but this was reduced to one penny in 1912 and thus the name. The Penny Bridge was to serve the crossings until it was sold to the city in 1912 and replaced by the current lift-bridge and causeway. The bridge is named for Sieur de La Salle, French explorer and builder of Fort Frontenac and deeded owner of most of the land encompassing the present City of Kingston.

Also to the south and east of the bay is the site of **Knapp Boatbuilding**, established in the 1870's. It sat on what is now DND land east of Frontenac Village. The Knapps had previously done business in Barriefield, and had an excellent reputation for building small wooden working and pleasure boats. In 1913, the Royal Canadian Horse Artillery stables were built on the same land. The structures were torn down to make way for Normandy Hall (1962). Excavation for the Hall uncovered several old vessels.

**The Montreal Transportation Company** transported grain from the Upper Great Lakes up the St. Lawrence River to Montreal, using barges and tugs and later steam-powered vessels. The company was owned by Ogilvie Flour of Montreal. It operated from 1868 to 1921, and owned at least 68 steamships and 35 barges. Over the years, they operated from four different sites: a wharf at Princess Street, a grain elevator at the foot of Barrack Street, a shipyard in Portsmouth, and their main shipyard on Anglin Bay. The shipyard later became the Sowards Coal and Fuel business, that stretched all the way to Wellington Street, now east of Frontenac Village. The site is currently the parking area for Normandy Hall and the Department of National Defense.

**Sowards Coal Company** was founded by John Soward before the First World War. Their slogan was "Sowards keeps coal, coal keeps Sowards". Their vessels brought coal for local consumption from ports in New York. Sowards were also co-owners of Crawford Fuels, as well as Maple Leaf Steamship Co., owning a large steamer named Padoris after the eldest daughter of the Sowards and Crawford families.

**Bajus Brewery:** "**Kingston can boast the first brewery in Ontario.**" We know that there had been a brewery on this site as early as 1793. By 1812, new brewery buildings had been built in the middle of what is now Wellington Street. The War of 1812 prompted a surge in beer sales, with the army buying thousands of gallons at a time. A new brewery owner started erecting a stone building to replace the old wooden one around 1835-40, including a stone section with a gable roof facing Wellington Street. The four-storey malting tower was built in 1857, and the portion that joined the sections dates from 1861. (Note the two beer kegs implanted in the east wall of the tower.) The row of iron stars beneath are to represent 12 Star Lager. The brewery was closed in 1922 and is now the Bajus Condominiums.

**The Anglin Bay Lumber Company** originally occupied both sides of Wellington Street north of Bay Street, which is the current site of the OHIP building. Anglin Fuels was located on the site of the current Leeuwarden Condominiums.

**Metal Craft Marine.** Boatbuilding has played a major part in Kingston's past since 1676 and continues to this day with Metal Craft Marine, founded in 1987, the premier builder of aluminum fire boats, rescue boats and work boats in North America.

Following the American Revolution, the British transferred their ship building from Carleton Island to Point Frederick, beyond which lay Navy Bay, a long deep inlet. Fifteen warships were built here during the War of 1812.

During WWII, the Kingston shipyards built 12 corvettes, two western trawlers and seven Warrior Class Tugs. After the war, 70 hulls were produced, mostly scows and barges. The yard closed in 1968.

**The Davis Dry Dock** was founded by Captain Robert Davis in 1867, in what was known as the French Harbour, on land north of Fort Frontenac. With the opening of the Welland Canal in 1889, Robert built a large drydock accommodating vessels up to 215 feet long, 42 feet wide and with a 10-foot draught. Construction was completed in 1892. The company built 70 steam launches and passenger steamboats and, in the early 1900's, built gasoline-driven boats and luxury steam yachts destined for Muskoka. The company expanded in 1895, becoming R. Davis & Son and, by 1905, had achieved sales of $50,000 and a weekly payroll of $500. During WWII, the company produced lifeboats and small wooden ships. Operations ceased in 1928. Of note, the Phoebe was built here as well as the James Swift, which ran between Kingston and Ottawa. (The restored Phoebe can be seen at the Pumping station on Ontario Street.)

**The Canada Dredge & Dock Company** moved its shipbuilding and ship repair operations to Kingston in 1931 after obtaining a maintenance contract with the St. Lawrence Ship Canal from the Federal government. They purchased the drydock, including a working shipbuilding and ship repair business at the foot of North Street from the Anglin Bay Company in 1933. The company remained active building barges, tugboats, and dredges for the next 53 years, until April 1986 when it closed its doors. During the war, most of the workers were teenagers.

[Today, the Kingston Marina is located in Anglin Bay and is managed by Metal Craft Marine. Slips can be rented and shower facilities for boaters and cyclists are available. During the winter, a bubble system operates to prevent the water from freezing around the boats moored there.]

**K&P Turntable**. Roundhouses are a particular North American invention, and a small four-stall roundhouse sat below the crest of Rideau Street near the water's edge at the foot of North Street. The turntable stood in front of the roundhouse and pivoted on a central point designed to reverse the direction of the engine. Of historic note, the turntable is now located in Wakefield, Quebec for the tourist steam train. The Ontario Foundry became known as The Canadian Locomotive Company and was billed as the largest locomotive foundry in North America. The Foundry produced five engines for the Grand Trunk Railroad in the 1850's. The engines weighed 50 tons each and could haul 500 tons.

The company was sold to Canadian Engineering and Machinery Company in 1864, but failed in 1878. It then briefly returned as the Canadian Locomotive Company, and was purchased by M.J. Hanley in 1901, who developed some of the most advanced locomotives on the continent. After WWI, the foundry built huge steam locomotives and the first electric engine in North America. The foundry shut down in 1969, and the only survivor of the foundry is the 10-wheeler John A. Macdonald, now housed behind the Tourist office on Ontario Street.

By 1970, the locomotive works had closed and, with the subsequent closure of the Kingston Shipyards and the Davis Tannery, much of the industry along the Cataraqui River ceased. The Canadian Locomotive Company became the Fairbanks-Morse Company, but closed in 1969.

**The Queen City Oil And Gasification Company** on Wellington below Rideaucrest is a limestone building designed by William Newlands. The building was built in 1908 for the Queen City Oil Company at 9 North

Street, and was later purchased by Standard Oil. The facility sold kerosene for lamps, and had a stable on the property for deliveries.

**The Molly Brant Plaque** is on the site of the land given to Molly by the British Government. It is just behind Rideaucrest. Molly Brant was born in the province of New York in 1736 to the Mohawk tribe. A matriarchal society, the women picked the chief and handled all economic matters. A masterful motivational speaker, Molly travelled with a Mohawk delegation in 1754 to argue against fraudulent land claims. The common law wife of Sir William Johnson, the British superintendent of Indian Affairs, Molly and Johnson had eight children. During the Revolutionary War, Sir William, a loyalist, tried to keep the Iroquois loyal to Britain. Upon his death, Molly took his place keeping the Mohawks on side and sheltering Loyalists. When the peace treaty was signed in 1783, Natives were completely left out with all their lands south of the Great Lakes going to Americans. For her loyalty, Molly was given a house, 116 aces of land, and a pension of 100 pounds a year. Molly was the only female benefactor of St. George's Church. She died April 16, 1796 at age 60, and its buried along with her children in the old St. Paul's Cemetery. (In point of fact, she is buried under the actual church. The plaque reads, *"Soldiers, statesmen, governors and generals wrote her praise. Her life was fraught with danger and uncertainty, but she survived this turmoil with dignity, honour and distinction."*) Molly Brant Point has been an industrial site for over 130 years.

**The Bone Yard**. Numerous vessels lie abandoned in the shallow water of the inner harbour as the area became a dumping ground for old vessels. Despite repeated political attempts to clean up the harbour, one hundred years later a 1994 archaeological study revealed 14 vessels just off the shoreline near The Woolen Mill's rear parking area. The wrecks are wooden, except for one metal-hulled barge (a propellor-driven steamer about 24m long by 6.6m, whose metal hull at some point was sheathed in wood as some bolts are visible) seen just off the shoreline. There is one wreck at the current entrance to Anglin Bay, adjacent to the DND parking lot by Normandy Hall, and an additional nine lie just off shore from Doug Fluhrer Park. There are three more farther north, and there is also a wreck south of Belle Island. At low water, ribs of many of the wrecks stick out of the water. Two are wrecks of vessels built in the 1850's and abandoned in the 1880's. But most were abandoned after WWI and settled in the shallow bottom. Some were raised and scuttled out in the lake during the 1920's and 30's.

Of note, during the Depression, poor urchins were encouraged to chop them up for firewood, despite the belief that they were contaminated with Asian Cholera.

**The Woolen Mill** produced cotton and wool, and was a major employer in the 1870's and 80's. It is now offices.

**National Grocers** on Cataraqui Street was built in 1950 with a K&P railway siding directly to its loading dock.

**Rowing Club.** The Rowing Club was built on land previously used by the Buffalo Ontario Smelting Company. The first rowing competition on the river was held in 1837. The Club officially opened in 1891.

**The Davis Tannery**. Leather-working had been in New France since the 17th Century. In the mid-19th Century, Andrew Davis operated a tannery producing goods for local furriers and cobblers. In the 1860's, Davis mechanized his production, installing steam power and machines. At the end of the 19th Century, the Davis family experimented with chrome tanning and, in the first part of the 20th Century, running water and electricity were introduced. The company had been established by Ford and Son in the 1860's, but was later owned by the Carrington and then the Davis families.

The site was chosen for proximity to hemlock bark used in tanning, and for good rail and water transportation. The factory produced upper leather for footwear. The Davis Tannery was one of the largest tanneries in Canada, and one of Kingston's largest employers. Production ceased in 1974, and the building was demolished in 1983-84.

**Belle Island.** A place of religious importance. The island was the site of an ancient First Nations Burial ground. Evidence of Native culture dates from 7,000 to 10,000 years ago, during the Middle Woodland period 200 -300 BC to 700-900 BC. During the period, burial ceremonies reached their peak. By the early 1600's, Iroquois settlements were strung out along both sides of the St. Lawrence River with tribes of the Oneida, Cayuga Onandoga, Seneca and Mohawk. Native population in the 1600's totalled over 60,000. The island is called Belle Island because of the bells of the Recollet Mission on the site.

# Key points from Chapter 15

When we think of the Kingston waterfront, we think of the land along Lake Ontario west, but there is another important and historic waterfront along the Cataraqui River north from the causeway. This was the industrial heart of the city in the early 1900's, with factories, the railway round house and turntable, oil and gas companies, tanneries and the drydock. Trains belching smoke came right into town to pick up lumber and coal, and three large grain elevators dotted the landscape as ship traffic up and down the big river and Lake Ontario carried on commerce.

# Chapter 16
# Land o' Lakes / Frontenac County

Another goldmine of opportunity
at our doorstep.

In the preceding chapters, we have presented why I believe that Kingston's heritage and waters are goldmines of opportunity.

**The same is true of the entire region...Land o' Lakes, South Frontenac and Frontenac counties are part of the Blue Belt, but so much more. They represent another goldmine of tourism opportunity but need to be branded and marketed.**

I attended a seminar of the region a couple of years ago, and two main questions were posed:

\*What attributes do we have to attract tourists?
\*How can we increase winter tourism?

I would pose a few more…

\*Can the entire region be promoted as a whole?
\*Can the region be branded for impact and awareness?
\*Is the region marketable?
\*What does the region have to offer?

The answers to the first 3 are all yes.

The answer to what the region have to offer?
A lot!

**Job #1 -- Recognizing what you have.
Job #2 -- Resolving to do something about it.**

# Okay. So what do we have?

* 5,000 bodies of water...fresh pristine, clear blue lakes.
* The 1000 Islands -- a place of staggering beauty. One of the world's great wonders, and totally undervalued and underpromoted.
* 1,000 kilometers of shoreline.
* At least 1,000 heritage buildings and the United Empire Loyalist story -- that of creating a nation. Again, totally undervalued and underpromoted.
* Bird watching -- 350 species of birds. The number one hobby in the world. And highly marketable. (American, Canadian and Mexican-bird watchers spend $250 billion a year on their hobby...$250,000,000,000!)
* The **Fresh Water Sailing Capital of the World** -- not one sign attesting to this world designation.
* The best fresh water fishing in Cabada: "Fish a different one of our lakes each week, and it will take you 96 years to fish them all." (American fishermen spend $40 billion a year on their hobby. We need to tell them about this unbelievable paradise for fishing.)
* Unlimited canoeing and kayaking in gorgeous surroundings. Huge draws for the young Creative Class.
* 1,000 kilometers of trails and bike routes.
* Three Provincial Parks, including 20 National Park islands in the Thousand Islands.
* Frontenac Park, the most southerly wilderness park in Canada.
* Kingston is located off a major thoroughfare that delivers a potential audience of 21,000,000 people a year (15,000,000 cars).
* The Camden Wildlife Reserve.
* Nine golf courses.
* The Trans-Canada Trail.
* The Frontenac Arch -- a UNESCO World Heritage site.
* 1,000 heritage buildings.
* The Wolfe Island Wind Farm.
* The finest water vacation lifestyle in Canada -- sail, boat, swim, fish dive, windsurf, kiteboard, bike, hike, paddle and row.

**An unbelievable list with the potential to be one of the great outdoor living/lifestyles in the world!**

Did you know that in the U.S., young families (the Creative Class) are flocking to Boom Towns for outdoor lifestyles -- hiking, biking, camping, canoeing, kayaking -- which sounds exactly like our region. Makes you wonder...

Here we sit with an enviable lifestyle, a plethora of outstanding resources, some of the best hiking in Ontario, Canada's most southerly wilderness park just 30 minutes away, every conceivable water sport, and 15,000,000 cars a year pass by.

**The missed opportunities are shamefully embarrassing.**
The region needs a brand identity, one that defines it and makes it memorable and unique.

## Land o' Lakes/ Frontenac County

# Eastern Ontario's Outdoor Playground

The positioning speaks to the diversity and adventure of the region, and sets it aside from all others. It defines the area's main appeal, and allows all the attributes to fit under the umbrella.

**So how do we accomplish this positioning?**

Establish the overall theme.
Develop a media plan.
Develop creative and material.

## Sample creative thoughts that bring the positioning to life:

1. Photo of canoe or kayak on the left, photo of one of the lakes on the right. "If you have one of these, we have 5,000 of these to paddle it in."
2. Photo of a backpack on the left, photo of beautiful wooded trail on the right. "If you have one of these, we have over 1,000 kms of these."
3. Photo of bike on left, photo of appealing country road on the right. "If you have one of these, we have over 1,000 kms of these."
4. A three-fold ad. Photo of fishing rod, then photo of a lake, then photo of a sport fish. "If you have one of these, we have 5,000 of these and hundreds of thousands of these."

The above campaign, because of its simplicity works across Print, Outdoor, and as 15-second TV.

5. Land o' Lakes. Land o' Wow.
6. Land o' Lakes. Our name says it all.
7. Imagine that you have 5,000 lakes to fish, paddle, boat, swim, dive and explore. Well you do! What are you waiting for? The lakes are here, the fish are here. Now you need to be here.
8. Unbelievable mansions, fairy tale castles, historic forts, spectacular cottages, quaint old towns, national parks. And you can visit them all by boat.
9. Water, water everywhere. So where are you?
10. Land o' Lakes...Land o' Fishing, Land o' Paddling, Land o' Boating, Land o' Camping, Land o' Biking, Land o'Hiking, Land o' Diving, Land o' Wow.
11. If water spots are your thing, do we have a vacation for you!
12. Like to fish-boat-paddle-dive? Then we have your number. So here's ours: 613-xxx-xxxx.
13. You can go for a walk or you can go for a hike in Ontario's most southerly wilderness park -- and, yes, there is a difference.
14. Think of it as the world's biggest Water Park.
15. Just north of the 401, but a world away.
16. Yours to Discover. Naturally.

# Opportunities:

## Produce individual Booklets
* Paddling Frontenac County
* Fishing Frontenac County
* Diving Frontenac County
* Hiking Frontenac County
* Camping Frontenac County
* Dining Frontenac County
* Antiquing Frontenac County
* Sailing Frontenac County
* Boating Frontenac County
* Doing Business in Frontenac County
* Bird Watching in Frontenac County
* Golfing in Frontenac County
* B&B's in Frontenac County

## Tours

Fall Drives -- A Blaze of Glory
Taste of Frontenac
County Heritage Trail Tour
The Artisan County Tour

## Extra Drives

Towns may have one attraction, but that is not enough for people to drive there. However, combining several towns and their attractions can create several loops. One town may have a great restaurant, another an antique shop, another an old working mill wheel, etc. The loops make it easy for people to take a tour.

# Winter Tourism

Winter poses a tourism problem for most Canadian destinations. But Canadians are desperate to do something through the winter to avoid cabin fever.

So here are some ideas to explore:

* Open a winter snow slide park.
* Develop a winter Rural Antique Ramble.
* Offer special winter B&B getaways.
* Have family sleigh rides all winter.
* Hold ice wine parties and taste testing.
* Stage a major ice carving and snow sculpture competition as a yearly event.
* Develop skating ponds and rivers in several markets -- play music, offer hot chocolate.
* Develop a Christmas Town -- Santa, reindeer, lights; Santa arrives every evening.
* Offer winter wonderland getaways -- seven course meals at restaurants in the county.
* Develop new downhill ski areas.
* Hold major Maple Syrup festival.
* Build an ice castle.
* Hold ice boat races on one of the lakes.
* Hold a 500-kilometer skidoo race.
* Hold a snowshoe cross-country race.
* Hold a beer on ice festival.
* Hold a yearly snowman-making contest.
* Hold hockey tournaments on a natural pond - how Canadian is that?
* Have ice fishing derbies.
* Hold dog sled races.

**Each town in the region picks one of the above and becomes known for it!**

# Key points from Chapter 16

Land o' Lakes and Frontenac County are a goldmine of tourism opportunities.

Let's review the numbers:
1,000 Islands
5,000 bodies of water
1,000+ kms of shoreline
1,000+ kms of hiking trails
1,000 heritage buildings
1,000 sunken ships
200 kms of a heritage canal
11 Provincial parks
1,000+ species of fresh water fish

Countless memories
Countless photo opportunities

# Chapter 17
# The Marine Museum Of The Great Lakes

Kingston has been a maritime town for over 340 years. The city became a major shipping centre, shipbuilding port and, after the 1976 Olympics, was declared the fresh water sailing capital of the world. And it all starts with the city's advantageous location at the confluence of the St. Lawrence River, the Cataraqui River and Lake Ontario. Kingston stands early in the maritime history of Canada, a story preserved and celebrated by the Marine Museum of the Great Lakes which includes the Kingston Dry Dock, for which Canada's First Prime Minister, Sir John A. Macdonald, laid the cornerstone in 1890. The Dry Dock was designated a National Historic Site by the Federal Government in 1978. The Marine Museum of the Great Lakes stands alone as the permanent reminder and reservoir of Kingston's rich 340-year maritime history. It is of vital importance to our national *raison d'etre and our history*.

**In other words, Kingston is here because of its waters.**

## First Settlement

In 1673, when Count Frontenac arrived on our shores, he chose the perfect spot for his fort and trading post. In the 1600's, and for more than 200 years after, the waters were literally the only efficient way to travel. One of the Count's men is reported to have said of Kingston's harbour, "it is one of the most beautiful and agreeable harbours in the world."

The original Fort Frontenac was hastily constructed of wood, but in 1675 it was rebuilt out of stone under the supervision of La Salle. The fort was primarily built for trade and later as a supply depot for other French forts along the Great Lakes. Large boats could access the site, unlike smaller ports along the Ottawa River which were only accessible by canoe.

Rivalries over the fur trade caused unrest among the Iroquois. In 1687, the armies of the Marquis de Denonville began a campaign against the Natives. The Iroquois besieged the fort for two months in 1688, and the fort was abandoned. It was rebuilt by the French in 1895 as a military base.

In 1696, the French mounted an attack on the Iroquois at the the south end of Lake Ontario.

During the Seven Years War, the British, under the command of Lieutenant Colonel John Bradstreet, attacked Fort Frontenac which was now viewed as a threat to Fort Oswego. Bradstreet's force of 3,000 men quickly defeated the 110 French soldiers at the fort and they were allowed to leave. The British took the supplies and nine French naval ships and destroyed the fort. It would lie abandoned for 25 years.

The fort was partially rebuilt by the British in 1783 as a military garrison and store house.

Note: A brigantine was built at Fort Frontenac to trade with Native villages around the Lake. LaSalle built a three-masted bark vessel called the "Frontenac."

## The British are Coming

When the United Empire Loyalists arrived in 1784, they chose to settle along the shores of the St. Lawrence and Lake Ontario for trade and commerce. This is an extremely important historic event. Up to this point in time, the area had remained primarily a French trading region. The arrival of the Loyalists changed all that. They came and created a nation based on British laws, British Parliamentary government and British religion: Anglicanism. In effect, the American Revolution created two nations., not just one.

The UEL were given land, tools and clothing by the British government. The Constitution Act of 1791 created the Province of Upper Canada.

## War Comes to Canada

With the outbreak of the War of 1812, Kingston became the site of the Royal dockyards and competed with Sacket's Harbor in a frenzy of warship building for supremacy of the Great Lakes. The War has been called The Shipbuilders' War, culminating in the construction and launching of the "St. Lawrence", a three-storey high ship with 112 guns and 700 crew -- the largest warship ever built on the Great Lakes. The HMS St. Lawrence gave the British complete control of the lake in the last months of the war. The ship, however, never saw action, as the Americans were deterred from sailing simply due to her presence.

Decommissioned in 1815, she was sold to Robert Drummond for 25 pounds and used as a beer warehouse. It was later sunk in 30 feet of water.

The war offered an ideal impetus for the marriage of cannon and sail. Amazing paintings exist of the great naval battles of the war, of which most people are totally unaware. The "Royal George", the flagship of the Provincial Marine, was built in Kingston 1809; it was 96 feet in length, had twenty two 32-pound cannonade, and carried a crew of 80 men. Commodore Hugh Earl was master and commander.

## The Naval Dockyards, 1728-1853

A government wharf was erected in 1763. In 1785, government stores were moved from Carleton Island to Cataraqui. Point Frederick was established as a naval depot in 1789 and ships began to be constructed.

The Quarter Master General's department had a monopoly on shipping on the Great Lakes, and transport schooners of the Provincial Marine were built on Point Frederick by 1792.

The Kingston Royal Naval Dockyard was the only Navy Base on Lake Ontario. In 1812, the Provincial Marine operated only four vessels armed with 20 short-barreled guns. After May 1812, under the command of Commodore Yeo, the facility grew rapidly. At the end of 1813, 1,600 personnel manned vessels counting 518 guns.

The Rush-Bagot Agreement of 1817 restricted naval forces on Lake Ontario to one gunboat. In 1818, Captain Robert Barrie built a stone frigate to warehouse the gear from the ships. The ships were auctioned off in the 1830's.

Closed in 1835, the dockyard was reopened in 1877 in response to the rebellion in the Canadas. Vessels were hurriedly bought and armed and manned by sailors of the fleet.

After 1838, the British government revived the naval establishment on the lakes and built the "Minos" (1840), a steam vessel, and the "Cherokee" (a wooden paddle-wheeler warship, which the U.S. saw as a breach of The Rush-Bagot Agreement). The dockyard was officially reopened 1845-1850.

## Shipping

From the mid-1800's to the mid-1900's, Kingston was a major shipping centre with large barges and steam-powered vessels calling at our port as they carried lumber and other goods to the world.

In 1846, the Hon. John Hamilton had the first privately-owned steamer (the Passport) built in Kingston.

In 1853, Hamilton ordered another steamer for his Royal Mail Line (the Kingston), complete with marble-topped tables, a piano, ornamental glass lights, carpets, and luxurious couches for seating his passengers. The Royal Mail Line travelled to Kingston, Cobourg, Port Hope, Darlington, Toronto and Hamilton. In the summer of 1860, the "Kingston" was used for the visit of Prince Edward. The Prince was in Canada to lay the cornerstone of the new Parliament building in Ottawa.

In June 1861, Prince Alfred, younger brother of the Prince of Wales, and the Governor General went up the St. Lawrence on the "Kingston". The ship (now called the Cornwall) was scuttled near Amherst Island in 1932 and discovered in 1989.

In 1901, Nat Davis of the Davis Drydock built a steamer launch (the Alleghenia) for Dr. John Bashear of the University of Pittsburg, and another (the Phoebe, named after Bashear's wife). The "Phoebe" was restored and can be seen at the Pump House Museum in Kingston.

The opening of the St. Lawrence Seaway in the late 1950's ceased Kingston's role as a shipping centre.

## Virtual Underwater Museum

From Picton to Brockville, there are over 1,000 sunken ships, many well-documented and a scuba diver's paradise. Some of the more notable wrecks are: HMS Wolfe, William Johnson, St. Lawrence, Katie Ecles, City of Sheboygan, Wolfe Islander II, Ricky's Tug, Queen Mary, Empress, Cornwall, Glendora, Monkey Wrench, Alberta, Aloha, Effie May, George A. Marsh, Comet, HMS Wolfe.

## World War Ship Building

Throughout WWI, six minesweepers were built at Kingston. In 1920, two cargo ships were built for the Canadian Government Merchant Marine (the Canadian Caster and the Canadian Beaver).

During WWII, Corvettes were built in Kingston for use in escorting cargo convoys across the Atlantic. "HMCS Napanee" was the first of twelve. From 1939 to 1945, three classes of ships were built at Kingston: 12 Corvettes, 2 Western Isles trawlers and 7 Warrior Class tugs. Two of the

Corvettes were lost in the war. The shipyard was closed in 1968.

## Olympic Sailing

In 1976, the famous winds of Kingston played host to the Olympic sailing races for the Montreal Olympics. Kingston was declared the Fresh Water Sailing Capital of the World. There are only a handful of sail race sites in the world -- Kingston is the only one in North America, and the only freshwater port, making it very special.

Six sailing classes of boats: Fin Flying Dutchman, Dinghy-fin, Catamaran, Tornado, Keelboat-Tempest, Soling. Forty countries participated, with 225 male athletes and one female, Beatriz De Lisocky from Columbia.

In 1969, CORK (Canadian Olympic Regatta Kingston) was established to host international sailing. The mission of CORK is to encourage and promote sailing and the training of Canadian sailors for Olympic sailing races, in addition to arranging sailing races, matches and competitions in Kingston, Ontario.

Ontario Sailing has designated the Kingston Yacht Club as an Ontario High Performance Training Centre. CORK YouthFest started in the mid-1980's, with two-day training events, seminars, coaching, and debriefing of young sailors. CORK has hosted championships for international classes for the past 36 years. Each year, over 1,000 boats participate, with approximately 1,400 sailors. Annual regattas are held in August and September.

CORK Olympic Classes Regatta is a high-performance event in which Canadians compete against world-class sailors. The third regatta CORK ONE Design is a competition for dedicated recreational sailors following "The sailing for life path". The final annual event is Fall CORK for Olympic and development classes.

The Kingston Yacht Club started in 1896 for ice boats and rowers, to encourage the building and sailing of yachts, canoes and motorboats. The first yacht built was the 21-foot Kathleen, launched in 1907; in 1908, the boat won the George International and the Bruce Carruthers Trophy.

The Laser standard will be used for men in the 2016 and 2020 Olympic sailing events, and Laser Radial will be used by women in the same games.

## Metalcraft Marine

Metalcraft Marine carries on the tradition of boat building in Kingston producing speed, patrol, fire, rescue and work boats. During the 19th Century, the site was known as Anglin shipyard and the Davis Drydock, which was built around 1900. In the 1930's, Canada Dredge owned the facility and built Navy ships during the war. It continued to build boats and did repairs until the 1980's. In 1980, the Kingston Marina began at 349 Wellington St. In 1996, they purchased 347 Wellington St. and the drydock, which became the only functioning drydock between Montreal and Whitby. The site has seen 340 years of boat building.

## The Blue Belt

Other cities brag about their green belts, but Kingston has a blue belt, as we are virtually surrounded by fresh water: Lake Ontario to the south, the Bay of Quinte to the west, the St. Lawrence River to the east along with the incomparable Thousand Islands (one of the most beautiful waterways in the world), the Rideau Canal to the northeast and, to the immediate north, over 5,000 bodies of water. If you fished or paddled a different one of our lakes each week, it would take you 96 years to try them all. Within a one-hour drive of City Hall, there are 38 lakes!

This water wonderland gives us the finest water lifestyle in North America. Sailing, fishing, powerboating, canoeing, kayaking, diving, kiteboarding, windsurfing, swimming. These are huge tourist and potential resident draws.

# Key points from Chapter #16

**Kingston has a 340-year maritime history of ship building, shipping and world class sailing.**

**Kingston is The Fresh Water Sailing Capital of the World -- Any other city in the world that could make this claim would merchandise this amazing fact. The strategic location of Kingston at the confluence of Lake Ontario, the St. Lawrence River, and the Cataraqui River was the very lifeblood of the city's being.**

**The site was first a fort/trading post in the late 1600's, with the waters providing transportation during the fur trade.**

**The UEL chose to come here and live along the waters of Lake Ontario and the St. Lawrence River.**

**During the War of 1812, we were the Naval dockyards for the battleships built for the war. Throughout the late 1800's to the mid-1900's, Kingston was a major shipping port. Corvettes were built here for the second World War and, in 1976, we were declared The Fresh Water Sailing Capital of the World. Today, the shipbuilding tradition continues with world-class fire and rescue boats produced at Metalcraft Marine in the inner harbour.**

Opportunity:
Our water story needs to be told! It is the "raison d'etre" for our city.

*"You open a book and the pages are blank. The book is called Opportunity."*

# Section 4
# The City

# Chapter 18
# Hockey: The Great Frozen Game

It thrills us, entertains us, and gives us national pride. It is our game.

Do we riot when governments raise taxes? No, we do not. Do we riot when the government wastes millions of dollars? No, we do not. Did we riot when Rocket Richard was suspended? Your darn right, we did...tore Montreal apart. Why? **Because it's hockey and it's important.** Did Canada come to a halt in the '72 series and hold its collective breath until Paul Henderson scored the shot heard round the world? Yes, we did. Why? **Because it's hockey and it's important**. What prompted everyone in a small town in Saskatchewan to get in their vans and trucks and cars and drive 1,000 miles to a midwestern U.S. town to dismantle and bring home an old ice rink? **Because it's hockey and it's important.**

Watch a three-year-old playing hockey in his driveway. He can hardly move the tennis ball, but when it dribbles over the goal line, the child will thrust his hands above his head in triumph. **It's part of our DNA.** Our childhood heroes wear skates. And we proudly display their names on our jerseys.

**But what does the average Canadian know about the evolution of the Great Frozen Game? Or Kingston's significant role in the game's development?**

Do we claim the first game? No, that event is lost to time and controversy. But we do know that Kingston and Kingston people were at the forefront, helping to pioneer the game and its rules carrying it forth to the world. We have been playing hockey for a very long time.

We are one of the Cradles of Hockey and Hockey's Hub.

We have an early puck (cut down from a lacrosse ball).

Four boys from Kingston scored Stanley Cup winning goals, and Jayna Hefford scored an Olympic Gold Medal winning goal.

We started the Memorial Cup.

We were the original home of the Hockey Hall of Fame.

Many of the pioneers of the game are from Kingston.

A hockey mask was worn here first by a woman in 1929, Elizabeth Graham.

The Queen's men's hockey team challenged for the Stanley Cup three times.

Lord Stanley and Sir John A. Macdonald were close friends.

## Details

Kingston was at the forefront of the game of hockey and its introduction to the world. Kingston players were many of the original pioneers of the game.

In the winter of 1843 -- January 3rd to be exact -- a young British soldier, Lt. Arthur Freeling, serving at Fort Henry, wrote in his diary, *"Began to skate this year, improved quickly and had fun playing hockey on the ice."* Twenty-five years before Canada became Canada. With that simple 15-word entry, Arthur set the stage for Canada's game. The Great Frozen Game. (And we have the diary!)

The Puck started here. In 1886, the Men's hockey team from Queen's University challenged the team from the Royal Military College to a game -- it is the oldest continuous hockey challenge in the world, now in its 128th year. Each team had seven players, and they used a square rubber puck cut down from a lacrosse ball. (We have the puck.) And we have one of the oldest hockey sticks, and one of the oldest hockey jerseys still in existence (worn by Guy Curtis, Captain of the Queen's men's hockey team in the 1890's).

Women's hockey. In the late 1800's and early 1900's, the medical profession of the day determined that the physiology of women was not suited to the rigours of ice hockey. Fortunately, the women paid no attention and the game flourished. Queen's women formed the Morning Glories in open defiance of the Queen's Bishop, who forbade women to play.

Today, over 100,000 Canadian women play organized hockey. And our Canadian Women's Hockey team have won numerous Gold Medals in World Championships and in Olympic competitions.

At the start of a Queen's women's game in 1929, the goal tender, Elizabeth Graham, skated onto the ice wearing a fencing mask to protect her face and some recent dental work. The Ice Hockey Federation acknowledges that this event was the first use of a goalie mask in the world -- 30 years before

Jacques Plante donned his infamous mask. Therefore, the father of the Hockey Mask is a girl. Way to go Elizabeth!

Kingston's Captain James T. Sutherland is one of the early pioneers of the game of hockey. He suggested many innovations to the game, including a blue line and 20-minute periods. While serving overseas in WWI, Captain Sutherland learned of the deaths of two of his finest hockey players, both killed in action -- Scotty Davidson who, just the year before, had helped the Toronto Blueshirts win the Stanley Cup; and George T. Richardson. Sutherland suggested to the league that a cup be struck in their honour, and in the names of all the fine young Canadian men who gave their lives for their country. The motion was passed, and the Memorial Cup was first awarded in 1919 to the Canadian Junior Champions.

The Queen's University men's hockey team challenged for the Stanley Cup three times (1895, 1899, and 1906) while it was still awarded to amateur teams, but they never won.

Kingstonians Doug Gilmour, Kirk Muller, Ken Linesman and Billy Cook all scored Stanley Cup winning goals. And Jayna Hefford scored the Gold Medal winning goal at the 2002 Olympics.

The Queen's men's team carried the game to U.S. colleges, playing in New York, Pittsburg, Baltimore and Washington. By 1888, Queen's/Royal Military College teams had progressed to actual team jerseys, six players to a side. In 1891, Kingston had four teams: The Athletics, RMC, Queen's and the Kingstons.

Kingston's Marty Walsh scored a hat trick in each of the three periods in the Stanley Cup final -- in fact, getting ten goals in the game and 38 goals in 12 games.

RMC vs McGill in 1892 was the first official interprovincial game.

By 1900, Kingston had 27 teams -- a lot for a town of only 18,000 people.

The West Point series originated when the commandant of RMC, Sir Archibald McDonnell, and the superintendent of the United States Military Academy (West Point), Brigadier General Douglas MacArthur, suggested a game of hockey between the two schools in 1921. After two years of exchanging ideas, the first game was played on February 23, 1923 at West Point. The Redmen won that first game 3-0, and a New York paper stated, "Army was beaten at hockey today by the Royal Military College of Kingston, Ontario. The Canadian cadets excelled the Army men all the way, displaying the best all around form seen here in years. Hamilton and the Carr-Harris's were the outstanding stars of the Canadian team. This game was one of the cleanest fought contests staged here this winter and was marked by a fine display of sportsmanship on both sides." In commemoration of the game RMC donated "The Challenge Cup".

In 1924, the series moved to Kingston, thus beginning the tradition of rotating venues. This was Army's first away game and, up until 1941, the West Point Game was the only time that Army played away from the Academy. From 1923-1935, RMC ran up a record of 14-1-1. In the 50's and 60's, Army won 15 of 20 games, closing the gap with RMC holding a 21-18-1 advantage. Throughout the 70's and 80's, the teams shared victories fairly evenly. In 1986, the record stood at 26-25-4 in favour of RMC. The series, conceived in 1923, is the longest-running annual international sporting event in the world.

## Kingston and Hockey -- The First Hundred Years (1843-1943)

1886 -- The oldest continuous hockey rivalry begins (Queen's versus RMC).
1890 -- Queen's opens their first indoor rink, sponsored by Senator Harry Richardson, at a cost of $10,000.
1892 -- RMC-McGill.
1893 -- The Kingston Limestones, led by Jock Harty, win the OHA Championships.
1895 -- Queen's plays for the Stanley Cup, but are defeated by the Montreal Winged Wheelers.
1896 -- Queen's carries the game to Pittsburg, Baltimore and Washington. Queen's women form the Morning Glories.
1897 -- Kingston Frontenacs go to the OHA finals; manager James Sutherland, star Jock Harty.
1899 -- Queen's men win the Crosby Cup and the Robertson Cup.
1899 -- Queen's challenge for the Stanley Cup, but lose to the Montreal Shamrocks.
1900 -- Kingston has 27 hockey teams.
1906 -- The Blue Line is introduced in Kingston; one year later in Ottawa.
1906 -- Queen's challenges for the Stanley Cup, but lose to the Silver Seven.
1911 -- Marty Walsh scores 38 goals in 12 Stanley Cup games (and a hat trick in each of the three periods of one game).
1914 -- Captain Sutherland introduces 20-minute periods.
1919 -- The Memorial Cup introduced.
1934 -- Don Cherry born in Kingston.
1939 -- Captain Sutherland proposes the Hockey Hall of Fame in Kingston.
1943 -- Hockey Hall of Fame formed in Kingston.

# Game On - A Canadian Memory

It was a game played more often than not, not on ice, but on the road in front of my house. Played with sticks, cast-offs from the real rinks and so worn down by the pavement that they resembled toothpicks with long handles.

But play we did, played in the days before portable nets, our goal two small mounds of snow, a circumstance that gave rise to constant arguments as to whether the high ones actually went in the "net".

It was an endless game, never interrupted by such trivial pursuits as penalties, time-outs, off-sides or line changes. Only occasionally taking a pause by calling, "Car!", a situation that would prompt us to move to the side, but just enough to let the offending automobile pass...just. This is such a part of growing up in Canada, that I have often wondered if an NHL referee could stop a game in its tracks by calling, "Car!" They should try it, just for fun. "GAME ON."

A game of frozen toes, frozen fingers and frozen tennis balls. These were the days before those insidious orange plastic road hockey balls. No, the real thing, frozen slushy tennis balls were the real thing.

Funny, although it was cold, I don't remember being cold. I think it had something to do with age and never wanting the game to end. But end it did, or at least that installment, with a parental call to dinner.

Sitting at the kitchen table, our tingling toes tucked under our chairs, our cheeks partly flushed by the winter air; partly by the excitement of our latest goal: "Man, you should have seen it, I let it fly from the other side of Burns' driveway."

I remember the daily routine of choosing sides, not by vote or arbitration, but by fist over fist on the stick. No fingers, no knobs. And the choosing would go on, back and forth, all the way down to John's little brother Robbie who, at six, was hardly the potent offense you coveted.

In hindsight, I'll bet that our street was no different than any other street in Canada. We had the kid (Keith) who always wanted to play goal. The kid (Ted) who didn't know the meaning of the word pass, let alone the word team. And, of course the kid (Billy) who insisted day after day, year after year, on calling the play by play while playing. Many times we threatened to beat him into silence if he didn't stop. We never did and neither did he.

None of us ever made it to the NHL. Few do. But we did all share a love of the Great Frozen Game. And I can tell you that the game is in good hands. How do I know? Because it is still going on, on my street.

However, there is one major change. Now, all the girls play, too.

**by Don Curtis**

**Opportunities:**

**Given the importance of hockey to Canadians and Kingston's long association with the game, a downtown Hockey History museum would be a huge tourist draw.**

*"Opportunities don't make appointments; you have to be ready when they arrive."*

# Chapter 19
# Kingston Downtown Ideas

Listen to the music of the traffic in the city
Linger on the sidewalk where the neon lights are pretty
How can you lose?
The lights are much brighter there
Forget all your troubles, forget all your cares
So go downtown
Things will be great when you're downtown
No finer place for sure, downtown
Everything's waiting for you

I'l be down to get you in a taxi honey
Better be ready by half past eight
Now honey don't be late
I wanna be there when the band starts playin'
We're gonna kick off both our shoes
When they play the jelly roll blues
Tomorrow night at the downtown strutters ball

* Downtown is where a community's stories are written.
* It is where our history was lived and still lives.
* It is where we are from.
* It defines who we are.
And it is vital to our survival and future as a city - a place that is vital and vibrant. We must protect it.
* Downtown is the centre of our cultural life.
* No one says, "I visited a great suburb."
* The perfect downtown is described as having waterfront, walkable streets, a farmers' market, ambiance, green spaces, historic buildings, a mix of old and young shoppers, entertainment and restaurants, bars and music...**in other words, it is us.**
* Other markets would love to have a fraction of what we have. We must protect and preserve what we have.

Despite decades of urban renewal projects, downtowns all over North America continue to be plagued by problems. Economic problems, perception problems and many more.

Online, you can literally find hundreds of reports on downtown revitalization, but few contain any new ideas, preferring to hash over old ideas and the same old weak solutions that haven't worked anywhere.

A recent walk down Princess Street revealed a number of empty stores. Empty windows with large lease signs scream trouble and scare away shoppers.

We had better be wary. Let's not lose one of the truly great downtowns.

Sure, you can go to a mall and get just about anything. **But there is no sense of place. No sense of individualness. No attachment. No personal service.**

You need to go downtown for the sights and sounds of the city.

**Opportunities:**

**1. No empty windows allowed.** On a temporary basis, let's use empty store windows to promote the store next door -- at no charge. Landlords would all have to agree, but the street would look a thousand times better.

**2. Develop an Historic Tour of Princess Street.** Most of the stores date from the mid to late 1800's and have interesting pasts. (See Chapter #9, The Stories and Storeys of Store Street.) A brochure is already done; it just needs someone to print and distribute it. Shoppers would walk down the street while referencing what the store was over 100 years ago. The idea promotes foot traffic and interest, and reminds people how special these old buildings are. You could put historic posters in each window regarding the date it was built. Not to mention looking up at the amazing second storey architecture.

**3. Develop activities for kids downtown.** In the tourist office, you will find two colouring book treasure hunts of downtown architectural anomalies that kids find and colour. The books promote families walking around downtown. The books were developed by the author and donated to the city. It should be given out in hotels and kid-oriented stores.

**4. Downtown needs it own newspaper.** This would promote sales, merchandise, festivals, sidewalk sales, coupons. Profile a different store each issue, print restaurant menus, etc.

**5. Have a "What's Going on Downtown?" section in the Whig.** This would appear each Saturday.

**6. Have more newer festivals.** (a) Military Appreciation Day -- Celebrate what the military do for the city and what they do for us around the world. We are lucky to have them and we should tell them. (b) French Canadian Heritage Festival to celebrate our beginnings as a French trading post, and the important contribution of Count Frontenac, Les Voltigeurs, Etienne Cartier.

**7. Develop more heritage tourism programs.** One of the fastest growing and lucrative segments of tourism is Historic Tourism, and no market can compare to Kingston. For example, Gettysburg, Virginia promotes a three-day battle of the Civil War and makes $95,000,000 a year. Old Albuquerque promotes its Old Town, making millions in the process, and they only have a handful of buildings and one old church. We have 600 heritage buildings and 13 heritage churches.

**8. Provide indoor parking for cyclists in an empty store.**

**9. Add plaques to historic stores.**

**10. Sell the bricks in Market Square.** "Be part of Historic Market Square." "Leave Your Mark." Have your name engraved on a brick which replaces a stone in Market Square. Cost $100. (Cost to engrave and replant = $20.) Cobourg raised over $250,000 doing this. All sales were by volunteers.

**11. Encourage downtown neighbourhoods to explore and celebrate their history.** It builds a sense of community.

**12. It is amazing that Kingston does not have a history museum.** A historic city with no museum to its history? Sir John -- the man who made Canada has no museum. The First Nations, Lord Sydenham, Molly Brant, the UEL, John Stuart, Count Frontenac, Sieur de La Salle. Not one has a museum...an unbelievable oversight.

**13. Hold Discover Downtown Days.**

14. **Paint the town.** Have local artists set up easels around town and hold a public auction of the works.

15. **Walk the walk.** Historic walking tours each week.

16. **Walk The Rock.** Public indoor walking at the KRock.

17. **Have a series of local downtown history stories.** Print in the Whig -- every house has a story.

18. **Put more hanging flower baskets on lamp posts.**

19. **Put more park benches in parks.**

20. **Build a fresh water fish aquarium.**

21. **Build a world-class marina.** One that is befitting to The Fresh Water Sailing Capital of the World. And don't forget to put up a sign.

22. **Build a Convention Centre.**

23. **Develop a deep water dock.** Refurbish the two deep water docks at the Marine Museum. Tourist ships will have a huge impact on downtown stores.

24. **Provide free buses after 9 PM.**

25. **Have a yearly First Nations Festival in City Park.**

26. **Create the 10-block downtown area as a separate neighourhood: Old Kingston.** Have appropriate signage.

27. **Produce a map of just downtown.**

28. **Promote heritage offices.**

29. **Rent the Empire Theatre.** On Friday nights, show only Academy award-winning movies for $5. And on Tuesday nights, show sing-along movies with the words on screen for $10 -- you will sell out every night.

30. **Downtown Indoor Market.** Among Kingston's many FIRSTS is the oldest continuous farmers' market in Canada. Its season is, of course, only a few months. But just imagine if we had a permanent indoor farmers' market year-round like Toronto's St. Lawrence Market or Boston's Faneuil

Hall. The facility would sell fresh produce and meat to downtown residents, but would also provide huge tourism draws. A restaurant would be part of the market. Organic green house produce would be grown on site.

**31.** Develop a Logo and Theme for Downtown Kingston. How about

### KINGSTON - HISTORICALLY HIP

**Downtowns are the only places where buildings have meaning and where there is a sense of place. Kingston not only has its own sense of place, it has its own sense of pace...a very attractive feature to people coming from Toronto, Montreal and Ottawa.**

People say, "Oh, I never go downtown." They don't know what they are missing. It is the best part of the city. I have nothing against malls; I go there all the time. But I go downtown as well.

* Show me a mall that has 25 gourmet restaurants.
* Show me a mall that has live entertainment and pubs.
* Show me a mall where the owner works the store.
* Show me a mall that has individuality and character.
* Show me a mall that has heritage.
* Show me a mall that has soul.

People also say, "But there is no where to park downtown!" Absolutely false. This is a Kingston myth. A few years ago, I went to the corner of Princess and Wellington, then walked a two-block radius counting each individual parking spot. I did this three different times a day on three different days. And in each case, I found hundreds of spots to park. **Hundreds.**

I remember the angst when the KRock was being planned: "It will tie up traffic, it will be impossible to get out of the downtown core." This proved to be absolutely false. It makes you wonder about the naysayers in our midst. They are destructive in the extreme.

## The Sounds of the City

The beat of a city is in its music and downtown. Kingston is filled with music every night. Pub music, concerts in the park, music on boat cruises, theatre music, acts at the KRock. And you can walk to all of them. Local favourites: The Tragically Hip, The Mahones, The Abrams Brothers,

Rueben deGroot, Spencer Evans, Sarah Harmer, Dan Curtis, Luther Wright and the Wrongs, Emily Fennell. Playing at: the Mansion, the Toucan, the Merchant, the Wolfe Island Grill, Tir nan og, the Kingston Brew Company, the Red House, Olivea, Brandees, Confederation Park, the amphitheatre beside City Hall. And don't forget the military tattoo and the War of 1812 Overture at Fort Henry!

## Hungry?

Take your pick: Le Chien Noir, Pan Chancho, Tir nan og, Frankie Pesto's, Atomica, Jack Astor's, Windmills, The River Mill, Chez Piggy, Casa, The Grizzly Grill, Fanatics, The Iron Duke, Sir John's Public House, The Pilot House, Tim Horton's, Coffee and Company, The Keg, Starbucks, Brandees, Curry Original, Sipps, Lone Star, Aqua Terra, Amadeus, Olivea, Megalos, Minos. And a lot more.

## Key points from Chapter 19

**Kingston's downtown is vitally important to the success and look of the city. Our downtown has all the assets and attributes of a boom town.**

**Kingston is repeatedly ranked as one of the best downtowns in North America.**

**The downtown is showing signs of losing businesses. Action is needed. Now! It is a lot easier to rescue a downtown than to rebuild it.**

**Downtowns are extremely important to cities. They define the city, its look and its true nature.**

**Kingston Downtown is Historically Hip.**

# Chapter 20
# Over 500 Things To Do, To Join, To Learn, and Participate In

Skating / Hockey / Curling

1. Rinks - City Hall. Supervised rinks - City Park, Victoria Park, McBurney Park, Polson Park, Woodbine Park.

2. Unsupervised rinks - O'Connor Park, Markers Acres Park, Cataraqui Woods, Henderson Blvd. Park, Shannon's Corners, Third Avenue Park, Molly McGlynn Park.

3. Community rinks - Springer Market Square, Compton Park, Ken Mathews Park, Hemlock Downs Park, John Brewer Park, Pierson Park, Invista Centre.

4. Ice rentals - Memorial Gardens, Centre 70, Harold Harvey Arena, Invista Centre (multi-pad).

5. Public skating - Centre 70, Memorial Centre, Wally Elmer.

6. Hockey - Church Athletic League, Greater Kingston Girls Hockey Assoc., Kingston Hockey Referees, Kingston Township Minor Hockey Assoc., On Target Goal Tending Instruction Camp, All Stars Hockey School.

7. Ice sports - Advantage 3, All Stars Hockey School, Kingston Striders Speed Skating, Between the Pipes Goalie School, West Kingston Skating Club, Senior Women Recreational Hockey League, Kingston Synchronized Skating, Kingston Skating Club.

8. Curling - The Royal Kingston Curling Club, Cataraqui Golf & Country Club Kingston, Ringette Association, CFB Kingston Curling Club.

Swimming

9. Pools - Artillery Park.

10. Swim Lessons.

11. Swim Clubs - Kingston Blue Marlins, Kingston Masters Aquatic Club, Kingston Synchro Swimming Club, Ernestown Barracuda Swim Club, Junior Barracuda Swim Club.

Field Sports

12. 55+Softball, Kingston Baseball Assoc., Kingston Lacrosse Assoc., Greater Kingston Softball Assoc., Kingston Panthers Minor Rugby, Kingston Thunder Baseball, Thousand Islands Minor Baseball League, Kingston Minor Ball Hockey League, St. Lawrence Viking Hoop Club.

Recreation Facilities

13. Artillery Park Aquatic Centre, Belle Park Fairways, Cataraqui Community Centre, Centre 70, Confederation Basin Marina, Grass Creek Park, Jim Beattie Park, Memorial Centre, Lake Ontario Park, Madoma Community Centre, Meadow Crest Community Centre, Portsmouth Olympic Harbour, Wally Elmer Youth Centre, Woodbine Sports Complex, Invista Multi-pad.

14. Wading pools - McBurney Park, Victoria Park, City Park, Lake Ontario Park, Shannon Park.

Hobbies / Social Clubs

15. Adult Rendezvous Club, Family Campers & RVers, Kingston Lapidary & Mineral Club, Kingston Naval Veterans Assoc., Kingston Road Runners Camping Club, Royal Astronomical Assoc. of Canada, My Soul Centre, Collins Bay District Horticultural Society, Communities in Bloom, Kingston Heirloom Quilters, Kingston Horticultural Society, Kingston Orchid Society, Pittsburgh Garden Club, Rideau 1000 Islands Master Gardeners.

16. Cadets - Royal Canadian Air Cadets Amherstview, Royal Canadian Army Cadets, Royal Canadian Navy League Cadets, Royal Canadian Sea Cadets.

17. Resource Centres - Community Living Kingston, Independent Living Resource Centre, Kingston Military Family Assoc. of Kingston, Learning Disabilities Assoc. of Kingston, Ontario March of Dimes, Welcome Wagon.

18. Seniors' Services - Kingston & Frontenac Elder Abuse Task Force, Seniors Assoc. Kingston Region, Pittsburg Seniors, The Step Safe Project, Community Senior Citizens Club.

19. Service Clubs - Air Force Assoc. of Canada, Girl Guides of Canada, 790 Dufferin Lodge Kingston West, Kingston Frontenac Rotary Club, Scouts Canada, Junior Chamber International, Kingston Lakeshore West Lions Club, Kingston Lions Club, Kingston Naval Veterans Assoc., Community Foundation of Greater Kingston, Habitat for Humanity, Kingston Archeological Centre, Kingston District Agricultural Society, Kingston Historical Society, Pitch In Kingston.

Volunteer Service Opportunities

20. Kingston General Hospital, Volunteer and Information Kingston, Volunteer Committee of the Kingston Symphony Assoc., Kingston and Area Assoc. of Administrators of Volunteers, Community Counseling Centres, Kingston Military Family Resource Centre, Ongwanada, Lennox & Addington Family and Children's Services, Breast Cancer Kingston, Hospital Elder Life Program, YMCA Volunteers, Kingston Interval House for Women and Children in Crisis, The Council on Aging, Extendicare Kingston, St.Vincent de Paul Society of Kingston, Independent Living Centre Kingston, Children's Aid Society, Canadian Mental Health Assoc., Alzheimer Society.

Cultural Groups

21. Agnes Etherington Art Centre, H'Art School of Smiles, Kids Play Musical Theatre, Kingston Arts Council, Kingston Heirloom Weavers & Spinners Guild, Women's Art Festival, Kingston Geological Society, Kingston School of Art, Summertyme Studio, Theatre Octave.

Dance / Music

22. 5678 Dance Studio, Flamenco & Spanish Dancers, Kingston Down Home Cloggers, Limestone Dancers, Pittsburgh Scottish Country Dancers, Rob Roy Pipe Band and Highland Dancers, Kingston School of Dance, Kingston Irish Folk Club, Clogging Classes, Salsa, Berengue & Bachata Dance for Beginners, Swinging Saturdays, Harp of Tara, Royal Scottish Country Dance Society, Kindermusic, Kingston Summer Music, Kingston Symphony Orchestra, She Sings, Women's Choir, The A Men Singers of Gospel Harmony, The Kingston Townsmen Barbershop Chorus.

Museums

23. Maclachlan Woodworking Museum, Military Communications & Electronics Museum, Murney Tower National Historic Site, Museum of Health Care, Penitentiary Museum, Marine Museum of the Great Lakes,

International Hockey Hall of Fame, Pump House Steam Museum, RMC Museum & Fort Frederick, Kingston Archeological Museum, Kingston Blockhouse Rideau Canal National Historic Site, Cataraqui Cemetery (grave site of Sir John A. Macdonald), Prince of Wales Own Regiment Military Museum, City Hall Tours, Bellevue House National Historic Site (home of Sir John A. Macdonald), Queen's University Archives, Fairfield Homestead Heritage Assoc.

Children's Services

24. Big Brothers Assoc. Kingston District, Boys & Girls Club of Greater Kingston, Girls Inc., Oakwood Pre-school Centre, Ontario Early Years, Queen's Infant & Child Development Centre, Playtrium Family Fun Centre, Sunnyside Children's Foundation, Extend-A-Family.

Education

25. King's Town School, Kingston Frontenac Public Library, Kingston Language Institute, Martello Enrichment School, Mulberry School, Scholars Education, St. Lawrence College Continuing Education Centre, American Sign Language Classes, Learning Disabilities Assoc. of Kingston, Loyola Community Learning Centre, The Reading Clinic, Maplecrest-Sempar School, Kingston Montessori School, The Earl of Pembroke School, The Kingston School of Art, Kingston Learning Centre Career Training, Academy of Learning, Career & Business College.

French Services

26. ACFO Mille-Iles, French Employment Resource Centre, Le Centre Cultural Frontenac, La Garderie Educative French Daycare.

Health Services

27. Canadian Red Cross, Hospice Palliative Care, Ontario Breast Screening Program, St. John's Ambulance, The Canadian Hearing Society, The Lung Assoc., Centre for Obesity Research and Education, Greater Kingston Safe and Safer Community Alliance, KFLA Public Health Walking Program, Ontario March of Dimes.

Fitness

28. Fun & Fitness 18+, Total Body Work 18+, Elginburg Fitness, Glenburnie Morning Fitness, Step & Aerobic Classes, Adult Fitness Programs, Strength Training for Beginners, 50+ Fitness, Strength Training

for Women, Pilates, Summer Lunch After Work Fitness, Kingston Body Management, Taoist Tai Chi Society of Canada, Boiler Room Climbing Gym.

29. Boxing - Kingston Boxing Club, Fitness Kick Boxing.

30. Cycling - Kingston BMX Assoc., Cycle Kingston, Kingston Velo Club, Queen's Cycle User Group.

31. Martial Arts - Academy of Martial Arts, Fang Shen Do Kung Fu, Impact Zone, Kingston Shotkan Karate, Martial Arts Planet, SMA Karate, Sydenham Innovative Martial Arts, Tallack Martial Arts, Kingston Kung Foo.

32. Gymnastics - Fort Henry Gym Club, Kingston Aeros Trampoline Club, Kingston Gymnastic Club, Loyalist Gym Club, Trillium Gymnastics Club.

33. Soccer - Cataraqui Clippers Soccer Club, Kingston & District Soccer Referees Assoc., Kingston United Soccer Club, Pegasus Athletic Club, Southeast Ontario Soccer Assoc., RMC Soccer Camp.

34. Yoga - Kingston Yoga Centre, Path Yoga, Yoga Samatva, Yoga To Go.

35. Hiking - Frontenac Park, Charleston Lake Park, Bon Echo Park, Cataraqui Conservation Authority, Cataraqui Trail, Lemoine Point Park & Waterfront Trail, Kingston Field Naturalists, Waterfront Trail, K&P Trail, Rideau HikingTrail.

Boating

36. Cataraqui Canoe Club, Canadian Power & Sail Squadron, CORK Sail Kingston, Kingston Yacht Club, Collins Bay Marina, Collins Bay Yacht Club/Sailing School, Confederation Basin Marina, Treasure Island Marina, 1000 Islands Kayaking Company, Brigantine Inc. St. Lawrence II, Kingston Rowing Club.

Cool Stuff for Kids

37. Pop Start (Artillery Park), Yu-gi-oh card club, Youth Cooking, Wannabe Chefs, Cooking Around the World, Sew Your Stuff, Cartooning, Babysitting Basics, Bike Maintenance, Skateboard Skills.

Clubs

38. Army/Navy Air Force Unit 377, Bridge Centre, Elgin Lions Club, Frontenac Rifle & Pistol Club, Kingston District Shrine Club, Queen's Women's Assoc., Royal Canadian Legion (#496, #334).

Golf

39. Cataraqui Golf & Country Club, Garrison Golf & Country Club, Amherstview Golf Club, Alton Moor Golf Links (Wolfe Island), Belle Park Fairway, Loyalist Country Club, Camden Braes Golf & Country Club, Colonnade Golf & Country Club, Evergreen Golf Course (Gananoque), Golf & Country Club, Inverary Golf & Country Club, Greenacres Golf Club, Landings Golf Course & Teaching Centre, Lyndway Hills Golf Club, Maples Golf & Country Club, Napanee Golf & CC, Rivendell Golf Club, Smuggler's Glen Golf Course, Wolfe Island Riverfront Golf Course, Westbrook Golf Club, Westport Rideau Lakes Golf Club, Quarry Links Expert Tees, Kingston Golf (indoor).

Camps

40. Junior Triathlon Camp, Camp Cataraqui, Grass Creek Camp, Summer Hockey Skills Camp, Sport all Sorts, Sportacular, Asus Camps Queen's, Science Quest, Queen's Reading Camp, Explore Summer Camp, Summer Archaeological Camp, Active Kids Kayaking Camp, Summer Christian Day Camp, Queen's University Campus Recreation Summer Programs, Explore Camp, Kingston Summer Music, Creative Station Summer Camp, King's Town School Summer Camp, Boys & Girls Club Summer Camp, Fort Henry Summer Music Heritage Camp, Hands on Heritage Camps.

41. Summer Neighbourhood Drop-in Centres - Shannon Park, Ken Mathews Park, Aberfoyle Park, Dunham Park, Cat Woods Park, Old Colony Park, Silas Stevens Park, Jim Beattie Park, West Park.

Miscellaneous

42. Cloverleaf Junior Bowling, Kingston Elite Cheerleading, Kingston Impact Basketball, Kingston Fencing Club, Sport Kingston, Multisport, Kingston District Sports Hall of Fame, Kingston YMCA, Power Play Centre, Queen's University Athletics, Sport Kingston, Kingston Tennis Club, Recreational Badminton, Recreational Volleyball, Beach Volleyball, Indoor Golf Lessons, Leisure Connections for Developmentally Challenged Adults, Knitting for Beginners, The Sewing Circle, Embroidery for Beginners.

LOYALIST TOWNSHIP ACTIVITIES

43. Senior Programs - Nutrition for Seniors, Photography, Guitar for Beginners, Bridge & Euchre, Bath Seniors Club, Loyalist Friendship Club, Interesting Years Club of Amherstview, Seniors Outreach.

44. Youth Activities - Babysitter Course, Junior Home Alone Safety Course, Go Girls Healthy Bodies, The Strong Self Program, Ultimate Paintball, Exploring Your Township, Ultimate Guitar, Loyalist Air Cadets, Amherstview Drop-In Playground, Amherstview & Bath Beavers, Cubs and Scouts, Girl Guides of Canada, Kingston Home Learners, Guardsman Baseball, Loyalist Township Minor Hockey, Loyalist Township Minor Baseball, Loyalist Minor Soccer Assoc.

45. Recreation - Badminton, Tai Chi, Recreational Volleyball, Bath Gardening Club, Rock Climbing Club, Go Take a Hike Nordic Walking, Run Forest Run.

46. Public Skating - W.J. Henderson, Tuesday Loonie Skate, Parent & Tot, Loyalist Learn to Skate, Seniors Skate, Sunday Afternoon Special.

47. Hockey - Adult Shinny, Loyalist Minor Hockey Assoc., Amherstview Jets Junior Hockey Club, Greater Kingston Girls Hockey Assoc., Brennan's Power Skating School, Hockey Head Start, Christian Hockey Camps, Kingston Ringette Assoc., Broomball.

48. Swimming - Public Swimming, Swim Kids, Red Cross National Life Guard Award, Junior Lifeguard Club, Canadian Swim Patrol, Adult Swim, Day Camp Swims, Triathlon Swim Training at Henderson Pool.

49. Adult Sports Groups - Amherst Slow Pokes, Ernestown Oldtimers Hockey Club, Kingston Lawn Bowling Club, Adult Volleyball, Odessa Mixed Bowling, Ernestown Ladies Slo Pitch, Ernestown Senior Hockey, Ernestown Slo Pitch Assoc.

50. Community Interest - Amherst Island Recreation Assoc., Amherstview & Odessa Block Parents, Bath Museum, Fairfield Gutzeit Society, Fallow Deer Reserve, Loyalist Community Sharing Centre, Odessa Agricultural Society, Wilton Women's' Institute.

51. Crafts & Hobbies - Bath Artisans, Bath Gardening Club, Collins Bay Horticultural Society, Family Campers & RVers, Kingston Division Canadian Railroad Historical Assoc., L&A Ridge Runners Snowmobile Club.

52. Dance - Canadian United Kingdom Dance Club, I've Got Rhythm School of Dance, Limestone Square & Round Dance Club, Royal Scottish Country Dance Society, Thursday Night Dancing, Killarney School of Irish Dance.

53. Fitness & Wellness - Fitball & Funfit Aerobics, Loyalist Tai Chi, Mushhotoku School of Martial Arts, Safe Stretchers, Tops.

54. General - Kingston Newcomers Club, One Parent Families Assoc., Save The Children Canada.

55. Boating - Loyalist Cove Marina, Brigantine Inc., Collins Bay Yacht Club.

56. Service Clubs - Amherstview Lioness / Lions Clubs, Bath & District Lions Club, Kingston & District Civitan Club, Maple Leaf Lodge, Odessa & District Lions Club.

Parks

57. Amherst Island Centennial Park, Waterfront Park, Back Beach Park, Stella Bay Dock & Park. Amherstview -- Amherst Drive Parkette, Centennial Park, Dinosaur Park, Island View Park, Lighthouse Park, Macpherson Park, East Side Park, Sunnyside Park, Willie Pratt Sports Field, Fairfield Park, W.J. Henderson Rec. Centre, Amherstview Community Hall. Bath -- Finkle Park, Hawley Court Park, Briscoe Park, Heritage Park, Robins Bulch Park, Centennial Park. Odessa -- Babcock Mill Park, Elwood Park, Dopking Park, Kilmaster Sports Field, Mill Creek Park, Centennial Park, William Street Park, Sk8er Park. Wilton -- J. Earl Burt Memorial Park, Wilton Playground.

*"Four things never come back: 1. The spoken word. 2. The sped arrow. 3. The past life. 4. The neglected opportunity."*

# Chapter 21
# The Silver Lining is Tinged with Grey

"Will you still need me, will you still feed me, when I'm 64."
-- Paul McCartney is 70 years old.

The Premise: Kingston should promote itself as the ideal spot for Super Seniors to retire after selling their million dollar homes in Toronto, Montreal and Ottawa. Kingston represents exactly what they are looking for.

Definition of Super Seniors - The first group of baby boomers reached age 65 in 2011 and are the wealthiest generation in history. The Super Senior group's average yearly disposable income is in excess of $100,000. With their million-dollar home sale in their pockets, they are looking for a hassle-free, traffic-free place to live. They are seeking ambiance and beauty, they are seeking recreation and culture, they are seeking a quality of place with a quality of pace. They are looking for a vibrant downtown, music, water, sailing, golf, safe streets, quality homes and condos, lower taxes and more house for their money. They are looking for Kingston...they just don't know it yet.

Kingston is unique. It is the only mid-sized city in Eastern Canada that has the ambiance, amenities, housing, services, assets and location to attract the desirable Super Senior target group as permanent residents. The city is lagging behind the provincial average in population growth, and the Super Senior group offers an alternative revenue resource to attracting businesses.

Fact: Report to Council, November 19, 2013 - "Kingston lags behind Ontario average growth." The Whig, December 7, 2013 - "Kingston's growth will lag behind the national average. Housing will be below the Ontario average." The Whig, January 15, 2014 -- "74% of the city's tax revenue comes from residential taxes."

Fact: There are currently 5 million seniors in Canada. This number will double to 10.4 million by 2036. For the first time in history, there are more Canadians over 55 than in the 15-24 age group. The 65+ age group comprises 14.8% of the Canadian population, and by 2041 will comprise 21.5%. [Kingston is now 16%.]

Fact: The Baby Boom bubble will last for the next 20 years. The group will control the political and financial agenda of Canada.

Fact: Spending by the 64+ group over the next ten years will increase by 61%, compared to the national average of 32%. Baby Boomer incomes are 55% greater than post-boomers, and 61% greater than pre-boomers. Super Seniors are the largest population group in Canada in wealth and political power.

**The Power of seniors = the Power of wealth = the Political Power.**

Both individually and as a group, Super Seniors taking up residence in Kingston are likely to bring with them a variety of benefits, including talents, social stability and experiences, along with their wealth and their positive impact on the economy. They possess a surprisingly significant amount of purchasing power, the result of steadily saving part of their incomes over the productive earning period of their lives to date, partly to save for a rainy day and partly to accumulate sufficient funds to maintain a desired lifestyle in retirement. Add to this money the proceeds of the sale of their expensive houses in Toronto, Montreal and Ottawa as they look to move to a city that has the proper Quality of Place with Quality of Pace.

Wait! I know what you just thought. Senior citizens drive up the cost of medical services. This is a myth -- they do not.

From the National Post, December 2014: "Maybe the aging population is not driving health care costs after all. According to the Canadian Institute for Health Information, the portion of spending devoted to seniors has not changed over the last decade. Despite growth in the senior population, the percent of senior medical expenses rose only 1.4% ( 12.3 % in 1989, 13.7 % in 2008). The dramatic rise has come from doctor costs and drugs across the whole spectrum of the population. The Health Care Aging Tsunami Myth: Aging on its own adds around $2 billion, compared to the cost per average Canadians, which is $8 billion."

From the Canadian Press, August 9, 2011: "Cost of aging population on health care costs are overblown. Neither the sharpest rise in costs, nor the larger share increase in costs was driven by the aging population but, rather, by factors that can be controlled by health care providers and policy makers. Aging-caused expenditures on hospital care grew by less than 1% and will be the same for the next 25 years.

From The Leyden Academy, January 2014: "Health care costs increased by 6.4 % 2008-2011; only .7% of this was attributable to aging. The remaining 5.7% was more people seeing more doctors more often."

From The Economist, 2009: "Money and mortality looking at Health Care spending 1970-2002, found that an aging population was responsible for only a very small part of the total increase in health care costs, accounting for 0.5% of a total 3.7% increase."

**The Senior population -- especially Super Seniors -- are not a drain on the medical system and are not causing the bulk of increases in health care costs in Canada.**

## The Incredible Offset and Social Value of Volunteerism

Fact: The value of volunteerism by senior citizens offsets any medical costs accruing to the group. From The Australian Study, 2004: "The extent of volunteerism is regarded as one of social capital, and thus an indication of a healthy society. The value of volunteerism in 1997 was $41 Billion, the equivalent of government expenditures on senior health care. In 2000, the 65+ age group performed 261.4 million hours of work -- the equivalent of 500,000 full-time jobs. Plus, the senior group is also the number one group for support of charities, the arts, live theatre, symphonies, orchestras, etc.

## Baby Boomer Wealth and Consumerism

Baby Boomers are not frugal. They have spent their lives buying what they want, and they have the wealth to continue to do so. In the U.S., the 55+ age group equals 21% of the population and 39% of the nation's household wealth. They have a net worth of $28 trillion, contribute 42% of taxable income, and 50% of all vacation dollars. Women over 50 spend $21 million on clothes annually, and are responsible for 70% of household spending. Adults 65+ own 6% of the net worth of all U.S. households, and spend $400 billion a year on consumer goods. They outspend young adults by 2 to 1.

**Political Power -- People will continue to vote irrespective of age and, in fact, older citizens are more likely to vote. This will make the senior segment the most important voting block in Canada, and any future governments will have to address the needs of this generation or be voted out of office.**

**Super Seniors are healthy, wealthy and wise.**

Super Seniors are the ideal target for increasing the population and wealth of Kingston. Here are 15 reasons why:

1. They have significant disposable income.
2. They own expensive homes, cars, boats, etc.
3. They do not take jobs from younger workers.
4. They invest in the community.
5. They are large users of financial services and home services.
6. They are the number one patron of the arts.
7. They are law-abiding.
8. They keep their properties neat, clean and in good repair.
9. They are well-educated.
10. They are technologically savvy.
11. They are the largest donors to charities.
12. They are the largest volunteer group.
13. They shop.
14. They hold the bulk of wealth in Canada.
15. They are the fastest-growing population group in Canada.

In a word, they are IDEAL. And Kingston is the perfect place for them. Here are 29 reasons why:

1. Kingston has the ideal balance of Quality of Place with Quality of Pace.
2. Kingston has all the amenities of a large city with a small town feel.
3. Kingston's housing is varied and affordable compared to Toronto, Montreal and Ottawa.
4. Kingston has outstanding health care (three hospitals and a Regional Cancer Centre). KGH is the only teaching hospital in Canada in a mid-sized market.
5. Kingston is the best place in Ontario to have a heart attack.
6. Kingston has available GPs.
7. Kingston has a vibrant downtown, vibrant social scene, and music.
8. Kingston has the KRock, the Grand Theatre, the 1000 Island Playhouse (in Gananoque), and the new Tett Centre, plus other smaller theatre groups.
9. Kingston has history and heritage with over 600 heritage buildings in our downtown core. Kingston is the historic heart of Canada. Sir John A. Macdonald lived, grew up and is buried in Kingston.
10. Kingston has abundant parks and is close to three Provincial parks.
11. Kingston has a myriad of sports and leisure activities for all ages.
12. Kingston is The Fresh Water Sailing Capital of the World.

13. Kingston is surrounded by fresh, blue water...A virtual Blue Belt.
14. Kingston has over 100 restaurants.
15. Kingston has Fort Henry and the Rideau Canal designated as Unesco World Heritage sites.
16. Kingston has an historic trolley, walking tours and 1000 Island cruises.
17. Kingston has an active seniors social scene.
18. Kingston has a safe, walkable downtown.
19. Kingston has Queen's University, The Royal Military College, and St. Lawrence College, as well as the highest percentage of PHDs in Canada.
20. Kingston has less traffic than larger cities, and car insurance costs 50% less.
21. Kingston is within a few hours drive of Toronto, Ottawa and Syracuse.
22. Kingston has an airport.
23. Kingston has good shopping downtown and 5 malls.
24. Kingston has a low crime rate.
25. Kingston is repeatedly ranked in the top three cities in Canada for most livable downtown.
26. Kingston was voted first for senior living by Shaw Direct, and third by Money Management Magazine.
27. Kingston has over 30 golf courses, 2 curling rinks, 20 ice pads and a Junior A hockey team.
28. Kingston offers numerous opportunities for later life learning.

# CONCLUSION

Kingston and Super Seniors are a perfect match. Super Seniors bring enormous value to the city through real estate purchases, income, volunteerism, support for the arts and charitable contributions.

Kingston should actively seek Super Seniors as future residents.

# Chapter 22
# Kingston2nd2none - Review

An outdoor & water lifestyle 2nd2none
Best sailing in North America 2nd2none
600 heritage buildings 2nd2none
A Blue Belt of fresh clear water 2nd2none
Kayaking and canoeing in 5,000 lakes 2nd2none
Fishing in 5,000 pristine lakes 2nd2none
38 lakes within a one-hour drive of City Hall 2nd2none
Boating in the 1000 Islands 2nd2none
Vibrant music scene 2nd2none
Arts and culture, symphony, theatre 2nd2none
Founding church of the Anglican faith in Canada 2nd2none
Home of Sir John A. Macdonald 2nd2none
Oldest degree-granting university 2nd2none
30 minutes from the most southerly wilderness park in Canada 2nd2none
The St.Lawrence River and the Rideau Canal boating 2nd2none

First Capital, First Parliament, First Governor General, First daily newspaper, First police department, First Prime Minister, First mention of hockey on ice, First puck 2nd2none

500 clubs/lessons/activities for the whole family --
and all no more than 15 minutes away 2nd2none

Over 1,000 sunken ships to dive and explore
from Picton to Brockville 2nd2none

*"Opportunities come and go, but if you do nothing about them, so will you."*

# Section 5
# The Summary

# Chapter 23
# Summary of Opportunities

The preceding pages have outlined a significant number of opportunities for Kingston based on our assets, particularly with regards to our History and Heritage and our Waters.

1. We are the Historic Heart of Canada. We are one of only four markets in all of Canada with signifiant heritage buildings. Promoting these facts will have significant impact on potential visitors.

2. We have 600 heritage buildings in the downtown core. Their beauty, daily use, architecture, original occupants and their stories are a huge potential tourism draw. History sells.

3. King Street and Princess Street offer unique opportunities for historic and architectural tours.

4. Thirteen heritage churches, including the founding church of the Anglican faith in Canada, offer a good opportunity for a niche tour and potential revenue for the churches.

5. A war was fought here and that, in itself, is a huge, potential draw. Add to that the connotation of the Shipbuilders's War, along with the fact that 15 warships were built here, and you have an a amazing story. The paintings of naval battles are spectacular, and would make a very exciting museum display.

6. The "HMS St. Lawrence" is a superb story, as it is the largest warship ever built on the Great Lakes.

7. The United Empire Loyalists came here to build a nation, and their homes still grace our city. Their legacy is the nation. Their story needs to be told.

8. The fact and presence of numerous sunken ships in Deadman's Bay, off Amherst Island and Wolfe island, are highly promotable and exciting to explore, not just to divers, as photographic exhibits would be a major draw. These photos already exist, as do the stories of the ships, a virtual underwater museum of the 340-year marine history of the Great Lakes.

9. The cast of characters from our history are extremely important and their stories should be part of a History Museum. A city designated as the Historic Heart of Canada should have a history museum. Sir John A. Macdonald, Count Frontenac, Lord Sydenham, Reverend John Stuart, Bishop MacDonnell, the UEL, First Nations, Molly Brant, William Coverdale and so many more.

10. More TV historic vignettes are warranted, attracting 1,000,000 viewers in 90 days worldwide. Current spots are Sir John and the Railway, Sir John and the Mounted Police, The Young Sir John, The Picton Trial, Winston Churchill in Kingston #1, Winston Churchill in Kingston #2, Charles Dickens in the Thousand Islands, Captain Michael Grass and the UEL, Lord Sydenham's death, Bishop Macdonnell and Regiopolos, Billy Bishop at RMC, the Old 18 at RMC, the hanging of Nils Von Schoultz at Fort Henry. Future considerations: Alexander McKenzie, second PM of Canada and a stonemason on Point Frederick Tower; Molly Brant; Commodore Yeo; Count Frontenac and Lasalle; Fort Frontenac; First Nations leaders.

11. Architecture tours -- niche market tours but important to the target groups.

12. Bird Watching tours -- Kingston has 350 species of birds, including Bald Eagles and Snowy Owls. This is the largest hobby in the world, with yearly expenditures of $250,000,000.

13. Plays -- a series of televised interviews with Sir John A. Macdonald, Molly Brant, Count Frontenac.

14. A proper hockey museum downtown would be a huge draw. Canada is hockey, and Kingston is the cradle of hockey. The Museum should be about Kingston's unique role in the birth of the Great Frozen Game.

15. Water, water history, water importance, ship building, shipping, recreation, water sports. Each is a huge story and a huge draw for tourists, potential residents and potential investors.

16. The Blue Belt is one of the prime reasons for people to live, work and play in Kingston. It creates a lifestyle second to none.

17. Frontenac Park, just 30 minutes from the city, represents a huge lifestyle opportunity to attract the Creative Class -- 5,200 hectares of land, beautifully-maintained trails, 22 pristine lakes for paddling and fishing. Most people in Kingston have never been there. It is the most southerly

wilderness park in Canada.

18. American fishermen spend $40 billion per year on their sport. We have 5,000 lakes full of fresh water fish. There are 38 lakes within a one hour drive of City Hall -- a huge opportunity to attract potential residents, businesses, and Super Seniors.

19. Land o' Lakes / Frontenac County are truly Eastern Ontario's Outdoor Playground, and should be branded as such. The tour and recreation opportunities are unlimited -- summer and winter.

20. Kingston is a city of firsts -- a DVD or booklet would be a popular item.

21. Kingston has a vibrant downtown and a lively music scene. The downtown should be branded **Historically Hip** to accentuate the uniqueness.

22. There are 500 things to do, join, and participate in. For all ages. And none are more than 15 minutes away.

23. We need a permanent downtown Farmers' Market. Kingston has the oldest continuous Farmers' Market in Canada. Build on this reputation and history with a large indoor market year-round, much like Toronto's St. Lawrence Market and Faneuil Hall in Boston. These venues would serve the downtown population as well as acting as huge tourism attractions. The market would have a butcher shop, restaurant and local farm produce. In off-season, imported vegetables and fruits, etc., would be sold under the auspices of local farmers.

24. Reopen the Empire Theatre on weekends. A downtown needs a movie theatre. The Queen's students need a downtown movie theatre. Downtown residents need a downtown movie theatre. The Downtown Business Association should rent the empty theatre on Friday and Saturday nights. On Friday nights, show only Oscar-winning movies. On Saturday nights, play sing-along movies with captions. The theatre will sell out every time, and the venue will provide a new fun downtown experience for all ages.

25. The really, really big opportunity: Convert the Penitentiary to a museum campus. The popularity of the two brief open houses showed the potential of the prison facility as a permanent tourism venue. But we can go a lot further. Imagine the Prison Museum in the rotunda and spokes, the Marine Museum (if it has to move), the Health Museum, the

Archaeological Museum, the International Hockey Hall of Fame, the Kingston Museum to Count Frontenac, LaSalle, First Nations, Molly Brant, Lord Sydenham, Reverend John Stuart, Rockwood, an Underwater Museum with photos and history of our sunken ships, an Architectural Museum, the War of 1812 Naval Battle Art Gallery.

Add the proposed Sailing Centre of Excellence, plus indoor and outdoor restaurants, and a large museum shop for all of the venues. All services would be provided under one structure, with plenty of parking and a single ticket for all venues.

Tickets: $20 per adult, $15 for seniors, $10 for children 3-15, infants free. Potential revenue = $1,000,000+ a year. It would be an experience unique to the world: Kingston Museum World.

Note that admission to Alcatraz is $40 per person, with 4,000 people a day touring the facility. On many days it is sold out. Their revenue is $160,000 a day, $1,160,000 a week, $80,000,000 a year. And it is hard to get to.

*** 

Kingston has everything it needs to be a boom town. It is a matter of communication and focus.

Kingston downtown is Historically Hip.
Kingston is the Historic Heart of Canada.
Kingston is the Limestone City.
Kingston is surrounded by a Blue Belt of fresh water.
Kingston is the Fresh Water Sailing Capital of the World.
Eastern Ontario is Ontario's Outdoor Playground.

All of these statements are positioning statements, and make us unique and marketable.

*"There is a tide in the affairs of men; when taken at the flood, it leads on to fortune." -- Shakespeare*

# Chapter 24
# Conclusion

## To recap -- Fifty great things about Kingston!

1. We are the Historic Heart Of Canada. *History sells.*
2. A war was fought here. *Gettysburg, Virginia makes $95 million a year celebrating a three-day battle.*
3. Kingston is the Fresh water Sailing Capital of the World. *There is not one sign proclaiming this world position.*
4. Kingston is surrounded by fresh, blue water. A Blue Belt that gives rise to the finest water lifestyle in Canada. A goldmine for tourism and economic development. *But never mentioned.*
5. We are a fishermen's paradise, a paddler's dream, and a diver's delight. Last year in America, fishermen spent $40 billion on their sport. *We just have to tell them what we have.*
6. We are just 30 minutes away from Canada's most southerly wilderness park.
7. If you fished or paddled a different one of our lakes each week, it would take you 96 years to try them all.
8. There are 38 lakes within a one hour drive of City Hall. *No 4-hour drive to your cottage.*
9. We have hundreds of sunken ships just off our shores, a virtual underwater museum to the maritime life of the Great Lakes. *Another goldmine of opportunity.*
10. We have 600 heritage buildings in our downtown core, each with a fantastic story to tell. *History sells.*
11. We are only one of four cities in all of Canada with significant 19th Century history and architecture. *And the only one west of Quebec.*
12. The War of 1812 was known as the Shipbuilders' War. Kingston built 15 major war vessels, including the mighty St. Lawrence. *Fantastic paintings exist of these battles. And amazing underwater photos of the wrecks.*
13. Famous people strode our streets: Count Frontenac, Sieur de La Salle, Molly Brant, Bishop Macdonnell, Lord Sydenham, the United Empire Loyalists, Reverend John Stuart, Billy Bishop, and Sir John A. Macdonald, the first Prime Minister of Canada and the father of Confederation. *They deserve a museum, and it would be a major tourist draw*
14. Land o' Lakes is truly Eastern Ontario's Outdoor Playground. And it can be branded as such. *Another goldmine of opportunity.*

15. 15,000,000 cars pass by Kingston on the 401 each year -- 21,000,000 potential visitors.  *Yet, we say nothing to them about the city, even though we have the capability via Information Radio to do so.*
16. Each year, hundreds of senior business executives visit Kingston -- Donald Gordon Centre, Queen's Executive MBA, alumni and parents of students.  *Yet, we put nothing in their hands to tell them why they should put a business here, or live here, or vacation here, or retire here.  A simple DVD would do wonders.*
17. We have a vibrant downtown, a waterfront, the 1000 Islands, a farmers' market, a symphony, a major entertainment and sports venue, and live theatre.  Exactly what people are looking for in a place to live.
18. Kingston is the oldest city in Ontario, has the oldest farmers' market, the oldest police force, the oldest daily newspaper, and the oldest Protestant cemetery in Canada.
19. Kingston is the birthplace of the Ontario Brewing Industry.
20. Queen's University is the oldest degree-granting University in Canada.
21. 73% of Kingston's workforce have post-secondary degrees.
22. Kingston was the first Capital of Canada.
23. The first Canadian Parliament met in Kingston.
24. The First two Governors General died in Kingston.
25. Kingston is the only Ontario city with UNESCO designated heritage sites.
26. Kingston has three institutes of higher learning, three hospitals, and the only teaching hospital in a mid-sized market in Canada.
27. Kingston has a Regional Cancer Centre, and the Cancer Research Institute of Canada.
28. Kingston is home to one end of the oldest operating 19$^{th}$ Century canal in Canada.
29. Kingston is home to 350 species of birds, including Snowy Owls and Bald Eagles...The largest hobby in the world.
30. Kingston is home to CORK, The Canadian Olympic Regatta Kingston.
31. Kingston is the site of the first Catholic school outside of Quebec.
32. St. George's Cathedral is the founding church of the Anglican faith in Canada.
33. The Royal Military College graduated the first Canadian military officers.
34. Kingston's King Street has 66 points of historic significance in a 4-kilometre drive.  *A fantastic potential tour.*
35. Kingston boasts some of the finest 19$^{th}$ Century architecture in all of Canada.
36. Kingston is Hockey's Hub, and one key in the development and spread of the game.  *Hockey is a huge draw for tourists, yet we hide our amazing hockey history north of the city where visitors can't see it.*
37. Kingston has Fort Henry.

38. There are over 500 things to join, do and participate in, all within 15 minutes from your house.
39. Kingston has the ideal balance of Quality of Place with Quality of Pace.
40. Kingston has abundant GPs.
41. Kingston has an active senior social scene.
42. Kingston has less traffic than major cities (and car insurance is much less expensive).
43. Kingston has easy highway access to Toronto, Montreal, Ottawa and Syracuse.
44. Kingston has an airport.
45. Kingston has over 30 golf courses, 2 curling rinks and 20 ice pads. And an artificial outdoor skating rink behind City Hall.
46. Kingston's Wolfe Island and Amherst Island are the two largest of the 1000 islands.
47. The largest Muskelunge ever recorded was caught at the confluence of the St. Lawrence River and Lake Ontario.
48. Kingston is regularly ranked as having one of the best downtowns in Canada.
49. Kingston is regularly ranked as one of the best places in Canada to retire.

**And, number 50:**

*Kingston is second to none as a place to live, work and play.*

KINGSTON HAS EVERYTHING IT NEEDS TO SUCCEED, TO GROW, AND TO PROSPER.

******

IT NEEDS:

THE WILL TO SUCCEED
A PLAN OF ACTION
A CHAMPION TO LEAD THE WAY

******

CHANGE THE ATTITUDE, AND CHANGE THE CITY

IT'S UP TO ALL OF US!

OPPORTUNITY -- GIVEN EVERYTHING WE HAVE, WE SHOULD BE A BOOM TOWN.

# REFERENCES

Chapter 2 - Kingston Facts =
Various internet sites.

Chapter 3 - The Brand =
Strategic Studies 2004 and 2010.
200 in-person, in-depth interviews with a cross-section of Kingstonians, conducted by Don Curtis.

Chapter 8 - The King Street Experience =
The Old Stones of Kingston, by Margaret Angus, U of T Press, 1981.
Buildings of Architectural and Historic Significance, Vol. 1-6, Kingston, 1973.

Chapter 9 - The Stories and Storeys of Store Street =
Queen's University Archives.
British Whig, article, 1909.

Chapter 10 - Kingston and The War of 1812 =
Flames Across the Border, Pierre Berton, McClelland & Stewart, 1981.
The Invasion of Canada, Pierre Berton, Pierre Berton Enterprises, 1980.

Chapter 11 - Cast of Characters =
Count Frontenac - Catholic Encyclopedia, Count Frontenac, by W. D. La Sueur, Toronto, 1906.
Count Frontenac in New France Under Louis XIV, by Francis Parkman, Boston, 1878.
Various internet sites.

Chapter 12 - History Moments =
Don Curtis/Chris Cochrane.

Chapter 13 - The Loyalist Parkway / Birth of a Nation =
PEC Website.

Chapter 14 - Kingston's Blue Belt =
Don Curtis, Ross Cameron.

Chapter 15 - Kingston's Other Waterfront =
Friends of the Inner Harbour.

Chapter 18 - Hockey: The Great Frozen Game =
Hockey's Hub, Bill Fitsell, Mark Potter.

Chapter 20 - 500 Things... =
Kingston Recreation and Leisure Guide.
Loyalist Recreation Services Guide.

Chapter 21 - The Silver Lining is Tinged with Grey =
Don Curtis, with the RELIKS (Retired Executives Living in Kingston).

Made in the USA
Charleston, SC
30 January 2015